## The Black Girl's Guide Mission:

*To empower women to go beyond any limitation, develop self-confidence through the knowledge and experiences of others, and use these resources as a blueprint for success.*

# THE BLACK GIRL'S GUIDE TO COLLEGE SUCCESS

### What No One Really Tells You About College That You Must Know

## Sheryl Walker

Bloomington, IN  Milton Keynes, UK

authorHOUSE®

AuthorHouse™
1663 Liberty Drive, Suite 200
Bloomington, IN 47403
www.authorhouse.com
Phone: 1-800-839-8640

AuthorHouse™ UK Ltd.
500 Avebury Boulevard
Central Milton Keynes, MK9 2BE
www.authorhouse.co.uk
Phone: 08001974150

First published by AuthorHouse    2/19/2007

ISBN: 978-1-4259-6065-0 (sc)

Library of Congress Control Number: 2007900531

Printed in the United States of America
Bloomington, Indiana

This book is printed on acid-free paper.

# CONTENTS

# WELCOME TO COLLEGE

Congratulations! You made it! You aced your SATs, wrote an amazing college essay, depleted your parent's savings account with outrageously high application fees, and have miraculously packed your entire life into a minivan. You have stocked up on a lifetime supply of ramen noodles, have said your heartfelt good-byes to family and friends, and now you are here ... college.

*The Black Girl's Guide to College Success: What No One* Really *Tells You About College That You* Must *Know* will help you to navigate those areas that are not on the university Website or in one of the gazillion fliers they handed out to you at orientation. I was just in your shoes a few years ago, and the good news is that I made it out successfully. Although every college student should have fun, study daily, maintain a high grade point average (GPA) from the start, and follow several other tips I share throughout this book, many black girls figure out how to succeed in college through a terrible game of trial and error.

If you ask the common person, "How do I succeed in college?" you might get the classic response: "Study and get good grades!" This response still leaves you wondering, *How do I study? And if I just study, does that guarantee I'll get good grades? How often do I have to study? Is this the magic formula for success? I thought students did more in college than just study, like get involved in organizations and study abroad?*

Much of the information I present is common knowledge for some; however, in the realm of higher education, blacks are still lagging. It's important that everyone does their part in assisting to reduce that gap. Consider this book to be your life jacket, providing you with the information you need *before* you take the leap into college. I don't want you to become one of the thousands of black women that say, "I wish someone had told me that information *before* I went to college."

There are many cultural hurdles that attempt to prevent you from reaching your highest aspirations. One example maybe an inferiority complex that developed over time based on the events that took place early on in your life, such as abandonment or abuse. As you will see, once you really get into the swing of things, you do have a unique experience in college and in life, being both black and female. This rings true whether you go to a *truly* diverse school, a Historically Black College or University (HBCU), or a school that is not so diverse. Despite the odds, black women have an impeccable inner strength and fervor that has been exemplified for centuries.

College is unlike anything you have ever experienced. In K–12, everything is outlined so beautifully for you, while college is not so cut and dry. College is a weird transition phase, kind of like puberty. People go through it, but no one tells you exactly how to deal with it. Remember the guy in high school whose voice cracked at the weirdest times during the day? And remember when things started to protrude from *your* body at a far greater magnitude than you would have ever imagined? (Your family always told you that you would inherit the family curves.) When it comes to college, try magnifying that feeling of uncertainty by one hundred! And guess what? There is no one in college that is going to hold your hand either. What adds to the mental confusion is that college students are under several misconceptions before they even begin, such as:

1) If I don't choose the right major or something I truly love right now, I will end up very depressed and poor.

2) If I just go to class and get good grades, I will be guaranteed a job making at least $100,000 when I graduate.

3) Well, because I was in the top 10 percent of my high school class, I am going to get a 4.0 and will probably be one of the smartest in the class anyway.

4) Oh, I can't wait for college because I am sure to meet my true love on the first day.

5) I know I should watch what I eat, but I've been this size forever, so I can eat the Philly cheese steaks from the dining hall, drink alcohol every weekend, and still maintain my slim 110 pound frame! Right?

WRONG! College is a whole new ballgame, ladies. To begin, let's wipe your high school success or failure slate clean. The fact that you were ranked fifth in your class and were editor-in-chief of your high school newspaper means something, but not a great deal now that you have already accomplished it. Those accomplishments were and still are fantastic. As a matter of fact, you should be applauded! However, you will meet tons of students that have accomplished the same thing, or more, on a high school level. Now it's time to not only continue that tradition of success you developed in high school, but to also step it up a bit and move beyond your past accomplishments. It's time to focus on the next series of challenges presented in this new terrain called college, and not get caught up thinking that everything in life will be a piece of cake. You have four years or more to acquire a whole new set of accolades that your parents can brag to their co-workers about.

For those who did not have the stellar grades or extra curricular activities in high school, that does not mean that in college you cannot have a 4.0 grade point average, leadership and internship experience, and have a great job upon graduation. This is the perfect time to start out fresh by completely revamping your mindset. You really can accomplish anything you set your mind to. If you believe in yourself and your abilities, you will succeed.

I want you to consider your definition of success. Now is this *your* definition or the definition your parents, siblings, or peers have defined for you? Success should be defined by your own terms! Success could be getting into the graduate school of your choice, graduating with a "laude" attached to your degree, securing your dream job after graduation, being the president of an organization, joining the sorority of your choice, studying abroad, or simply trying your very best and graduating on time. Never let anyone else's definition of success be your own! Likewise, never let falling short of one goal impede you from altering your goals and pursuing others full force.

So are you ready? College is so exciting. You are embarking on one of the best moments of your life. Have you ever noticed that whether a person finishes college or not, you never hear them say, "I regret going to college." You might hear them say, "I wish I had the opportunity to go to college," or "I wish I had never dropped out of college." Once you get the education, degree, and experience, no one can take that accomplishment away from you. You can always leverage that piece of paper above your peers that did not graduate from college.

Surprisingly, the majority of what you learn in college is outside of the classroom, but your degree has the *possibility* to grant you access to a world you may have never imagined. I emphasize the word *possibility* because it is up to you to take the education you acquire and use it as a catalyst to open up the doors of opportunity. It doesn't matter what college you are currently attending; the sky is the limit to where this experience can take you.

I want you to promise me one thing—that you will give some of the information I present in this book some serious consideration. Since I know how some of you may have limited attention spans, I have recapped some of the important points in a *So What Did You Learn?* feature at the end of each chapter. I have also included a few *Side Notes* and one *Homework Assignment*.

Before you begin your journey through these critical years, let's talk about an important concept you must adopt in your life from here on out: goal setting. **A goal serves as the road map to the fabulous life you have always envisioned!** Goals will keep you focused and headed in the right direction. Instead of progressing through life aimlessly, always aspire to reach your goals and be the best you can possibly be. I want your goals to be long-term, such as becoming a teacher after you graduate. Your goals should be short-term, like getting a 4.0 GPA for the semester. Your goals can be spiritual, like attending church at least once a month, or personal, like having a fitness goal to work out at least four times a week. I want you to set goals for all the areas of your life you feel are appropriate, but make sure these goals are specific and have a time element to them. For example, you may want to achieve a goal by the end of the academic year. Put these goals somewhere you can see and refer to daily, whether they are on your wall or in a journal.

Along with these goals, I want you to write down the steps (mini goals) you will have to take to reach these goals and the time frame in which you want to accomplish them as well. For example, your goal maybe to get an A in a particular class, so your incremental goals might be to study for six hours daily, or to attend your professors' office hours once a week. **Be sure to evaluate and update your goals from time to time, and never be afraid to alter or completely delete a goal.**

So, let's take some time to write down your goals. I will be here waiting for you to come back …

1. _____

2. _____

3. _____

4. _____

5. _____

You should still be writing. Don't skip this step. It is very important! Really take your time.

6. _____

7. _____

8. _____

9. _____

10. _____

Okay, so now that you have written down your goals, let's get started on those highly critical first days! But before you go, remember what I covered:

- **Success should be defined by your own terms.**
- **You really can accomplish anything you set your mind to.**
- **Set goals, but be willing to revamp these goals from time to time.**

Oh, one more thing before you begin. Let me explain who I am for those of you wondering why there is no Dr. in front of my name.

## So what makes *you* an expert in this field?

I'm no expert and I don't have a PhD on the subject, but I just went through what you are embarking on and was successful, based on my own terms of success. I was a Resident Assistant (RA), which means I was a counselor, peer mediator, and campus resource to over one hundred students. Throughout my two and a half year term, I lived in a suite with a total of twelve black girls, listening to their issues and helping them solve their problems. No, I have not studied the "science" behind the black girl's college experience. That is not the angle I'm taking. I want you to know the real deal, what to expect from the start, and how best to prepare yourself for a successful college experience.

Most of the things I present to you are applicable to all college students, like the first days and having fun. Then there are things that you know about, but may not realize how critical they are, like maintaining a high GPA from the start or getting an internship as soon as you can. There are also things like combating feelings of inferiority, which hit close to home for many girls of color.

I had to deal with some of these issues and so did many of my friends, peers, and residents. We often questioned, *Why didn't anyone tell us what college was really like?* College is fun, but not when you just got a C on an exam because instead of studying the night before, you were up crying after you saw Kevin walking around campus with Kim. Surprisingly, college becomes much more than classes and grades.

After graduating, I had far too many "shoulda, coulda, woulda" conversations with college graduates for me *not* to write this book. Why let generation after generation of black girls continue to have to figure it all out alone? I wrote this book based on my own experiences and those of my black female peers. This book is written with a voice and tone that I hope you can understand, relate to, and learn from. So when I refer to "we" and "us" throughout the course of this book, I am talking to you. I am talking to us: black females.

What if you are a non-traditional student? What if you are a much older student? A commuter student? Or from a home where life isn't so easy and fun? What if you have to juggle a job or two to make ends meet, or take care of a young child or older parent, all while trying to earn your degree? How does this book still apply to you? The challenge will be learning how to balance your personal responsibilities while making the most of your college experience. This will be no walk in the park, but some of the best students I have encountered are the ones who have more at stake, such as family members that are relying on them to be successful or people that have been expected to fail their entire lives. You should still have fun, maintain a high GPA, study daily, choose the right major for you, combat feelings of inferiority, get mentors, and even try to do a short study abroad program. This book totally applies to you and I don't want you to allow your current circumstances to prevent you from taking full advantage of your student status and the resources available to you.

There are certain things that I don't get into full detail about, like financial aid and scholarships. Why? Because there are many books and Websites on these topics and each campus has a financial aid office that will give you a plethora of information on these subjects. This book is for what no one *really* tells you about college, like navigating some of the areas that aren't so crystal clear in the beginning.

Life becomes a little easier when you don't have to figure out *everything* on your own. Millions of black women have graduated from college and have been successful, but having a heads-up on how to make it through successfully can only increase the population of black female college graduates. By taking the advice presented in this book, at least when you go through your obstacles, you will know that you are not alone. There are tons of girls out there in college going through the exact same thing. With the right support, **you will excel and accomplish whatever you set your mind to.**

So here's to you and the great things you know you can do!

*Sheryl*

# THE FIRST DAYS:
# TAKE ADVANTAGE OF THEM!

**Golden Rule**: As you conquer the first couple of weeks of college, keep this book in a very safe and accessible place.

**First Day Commandments: Thou shall …**

1. **Beat the Rush.** Move in early with many helpers (such as your brother, sister, and/or cousin(s)). You don't have to bring *all* of your family members, but a few extra hands help a great deal. If you are living in one of the traditional high-rise dormitories that house new freshmen, you may be sharing the elevator with hundreds of other students that are moving in on the very same day. It is probably the end of August and extremely hot outside. Although living on the first few floors eases the frustrations of moving in, lugging all your belongings in

and out can get very strenuous, regardless of what floor you live on. Try to move in as early as you can! The earlier in the day you move in, the cooler the temperature will be and the fewer amount of people occupying the elevators. You will be making several trips to the minivan, and to the store to buy a shower caddy and cinder blocks to raise the height of your bed to stick stuff underneath, if you have not already purchased those items. Eager helpers make this process a lot more bearable.

**Side Note #1:** Although the campus cleaning crew does a thorough job cleaning the room prior to your arrival, there is nothing wrong with doing a little cleaning of the mattress and the bathroom (if you have your own).

**Side Note #2:** Don't bring anything that can start a fire such as candles or a hotplate. Your school will probably have rules banning the usage of these items.

**Side Note #3:** If you are traveling very far to college, you do not need to buy everything before you get there. This will take up lots of room in the car and is inconvenient if you are flying. What you can do is bring your essentials to school, such as clothing and personal mementos, and go shopping for food and other dorm items once you get there. There are books and Websites out there that will tell you what to bring to college; however, as a warning, you *will* over pack. Begin with the necessities and then see what else you will have room for.

**2. Attend as many freshmen "getting to know you/ice breaker/team builder/floor meeting/meet and greet"** events as you can. Now if you miss a couple of these events, do not despair. You were not intended to meet all 40,000 students in one day or over the next four years. This is a great time to meet and mingle with other students, get to know your floormates, and locate the campus cultural center and gym (in due time you will have to work off that freshman fifteen). You can also locate the performing arts center, student union, book store, and other key campus locations together. Look out for the meet-and-greet sessions offered by the Black Student Union and any other organizations related to your ethnicity (like the Caribbean Student Association and the African Student Association). Also consider the sessions sponsored by religious based groups (like a Christian or Muslim group— but be careful of some religious groups that appear extra friendly and inviting at first in an attempt to lure you into their fellowship. There is a possibility that they may be a cult or other dangerous group). Hopefully you took full advantage of freshman orientation and met other students there. If you have, you can attend some of the "getting to know you" sessions with them as well.

Also, do not rule out the informal mingling sessions, such as exploring the new city with your floormates or joining a group of students that are already sitting in the student union chatting or playing spades. (There is a high chance that you will become a spades addict, so it's best that you get the art of spades down pact as early as you can.) Keep in mind that most freshmen are feeling the same weird new awkwardness and are very warm and inviting for the first few days, so take advantage of this overly-friendly behavior while it lasts. Be bold and introduce yourself. Perhaps you will make a friend that can accompany you to more "getting to know you/ice breaker" sessions. Don't feel obligated to commit to one group of friends you make and don't rule people out based on first impressions. Meet lots of people and be sure to write down their dorm room and phone numbers!

**Side Note #4:** Do not feel obligated to hang out with your parents during move in days. You have relationships to build here! They will be okay on their own for some parts of the day.

**3. Talk to an upperclassman about your schedule.** This could potentially be a great time to formulate ideas on classes you may have some doubts about and get other students' opinions. Some classes look good on paper but then take a miracle to pass with a decent grade. Just about any upperclassman you meet should be able to give you advice on what classes and professors to avoid and what classes and professors to take, and they might even give you their old books! However, even with this tactic, you will experience horrible classes and professors, but at least this method should allow you to keep this to a minimum. I would still double-check the information an upperclassman gives you with another source. Many universities have a Website where students have the opportunity to rate their professors and leave comments about the class. If you check the Website and it is considered a good class and professor, or you get the same response from more than one upperclassman, then I would sign up for that class.

Once you attend class on the first day, review the syllabus. (FYI: A syllabus is a sheet of paper handed out on the first few days of class that outlines the course, including the topics covered, quiz and exam dates, and how your final grade is computed.) Once you have the syllabus, try to gauge if this class is the best fit for you. You may or may not be able to do this based on the intro lecture. That is why it is good to talk to a few people beforehand so you know exactly what you're getting into. Also, be sure to write down their recommendations for future semesters.

**Side Note #5:** An upperclassman may even give you advice on who you should make an extra effort to get to know better. It might be the dean, assistant dean, or someone else with authority in your school who you might have to kiss up to a bit to get ahead.

**Side Note #6:** If your class is mandatory for your major, you may want to stick with this class, especially if this is the only professor who teaches this course. If the class is mandatory, at some point in your college curriculum you will have to pass it. It's not the best habit to keep pushing off classes. Most of the time, there are certain classes intended for you to take during your freshman year, a few more your sophomore year, all the way up until your senior year.

You may think your schedule is pretty much solidified at this point, but do remember that the blurb that accompanies the class you think you will love may turn out to be the complete opposite. For example, you sign up for a philosophy class thinking you will be able to debate on issues like abortion and euthanasia, when in reality you never open your mouth during a lecture or discussion and sit there learning a bunch of philosophical theories that are of no interest to you.

The unfortunate news is that not all college advisors are as skilled with assisting in class selection as we'd all like them to be. Also, advisors usually haven't taken the classes they recommend, so they have no real idea what the classes are really like unless they have been an advisor for a while and have heard students saying good things about particular classes and professors. Many advisors have only been advisors for a short period of time. You should still be proactive and schedule your appointment with them anyway. They do help you to figure out if you have fulfilled certain course requirements in an attempt for you to graduate on time. For example, even though you are a criminal justice major, you may still have to take a science lab and your advisor will most likely bring that to your attention.

**Side Note #7**—totally off subject: If you meet an upperclassman who happens to have a really nice hairstyle, ask her if she knows any good local hair salons and write down the names and locations. If you don't have a car and this is a new city for you, be sure to ask about the public transportation system that will assist you in getting there. It may take some time to find a salon that you love. Another option if you are a little short on cash is to figure out which girls on campus do hair for low prices.

**4. Walk around campus and see where your classes are generally located and be sure to get a map before you take this trip.** Soak in as much of the campus as you can. It may seem huge and unconquerable now, but in no time you'll know it like the back of your hand. Also, **explore the surrounding town.** Locate important spots like supermarkets, some of the local eateries, and the nearest tea and coffee shop. Hopefully on your first day of class there will be people on campus helping students to find their classes.

5. **Buy your books used!** In college, buying brand-new books is not only expensive, but a waste of money. Books can potentially run you around $200 each. Buying used books is much cheaper! You must get to the campus book store as early as possible before classes begin to get the best selection of used books and avoid the extremely long lines. You may want to try to purchase your books as early as three weeks prior to the start of classes. Be sure to comparison shop between the various campus bookstores and online booksellers.

You will most likely *never* use these books again after the semester is over. After you finish taking your finals, you will sell your books back to the bookstore and you usually get (if you are lucky), a third of what you paid for them. After you sell your books back to the bookstore, they raise the prices and resell them to students the following semester and continue to rake in the dough. You can also try reselling your books to Websites that buy and sell used textbooks.

Side Note #8: Pay attention to the textbook edition. Usually authors change only a few words in a textbook and keep the overall content the same, so that the used version of the book can no longer be resold by the bookstore. This forces students to buy brand new books. Authors and publishers want to continuously make money from textbooks sales. Seek out students that are willing to buy an old edition of a textbook.

In future semesters, consider book swapping with another student or going to the class on the first day and selling your old textbook to a student taking the class that semester. Selling your book using this method will get you a greater return than if you were to sell it to the bookstore.

I want to make something very clear: No matter how tight money is, you should make it a point to buy your textbooks. Having your textbooks is critical to getting good grades in your classes. You can consider checking a textbook out at the library if this option is available. You will have to get to the library very early. This option is only for those times that are extremely hard financially and there is absolutely no way you can afford a particular book. You can also see if the professor placed a copy of the book on reserve at the library. This means no one can totally check the book out of the library; you can only use it for a few hours within the library, and must then return it to the circulation desk so that other students can use this book as well.

**Side Note #9:** While in the bookstore, pick up an academic planner. As soon as you get your syllabus, you will need a planner to write down important dates such as quizzes, exams, and when your papers will be due.

**Side Note #10:** Keep your book receipts in case you end up switching out of a particular class and need to return the books.

**6. Get to know your roommate(s) and compromise** (but don't get pushed over). The "don't get pushed over" part of this commandment does not mean that you should go into the room on defense mode, because your roommate could be very accommodating; however, don't become so overly accommodating that you end up inconveniencing yourself. For example, don't be forced to have the smaller closet if you did not get the bed closest to the window.

Also, don't go into a roommate situation worrying about all the potential roommate conflicts. You will be able to handle it. If you are in a triple or quad, you will have to juggle two or three different personalities, but remain open and calm.

Many students grew up with their own bedrooms and now here you are sharing a room with a stranger! As unpleasant as this sounds, this is just a readjustment period and there are definite perks. For one, college can seem overwhelming in the beginning and if your roommate is a cool person, you can help each other figure things out and she can end up being one of your closest friends. Some of you may love your roommate. Others will have plenty of roommate horror stories to share with your family and friends over winter break. You may be a neat freak and your roommate is a slob. Your roommate can be extra weird and stay in the room all the time, use drugs, refuse to shower, lock you out of your own room, have her boyfriend practically living in the room, have all the players from the football team in and out of the room all the time, or perhaps she won't even talk to you at all. If that's the case, you should discuss the issues with her and try to reach a compromise. Seek out the Resident Assistant if progress is not being made.

The good thing is that most schools have a great Resident Life Department with people that have dealt with every roommate conflict that you could ever imagine. Within the first two weeks of your first semester, your RA should come around with roommate agreements. (If they don't, create your own agreement in writing.) A roommate agreement outlines rules about sharing items, guests, studying in your room, rules for locking the door, and other issues that may pop up down the line. Don't be scared or intimidated to speak up and set ground rules.

If the issue you are both having relates to an aspect of her personality, you may have to just accept her for who she is and tolerate her behavior. You have to understand that you are not going to change a habit that is already ingrained in a person. You may have to let some things go and still be a nice and cordial person. I'm almost positive you have some habits your roommate could live without as well. Learn to have a mutual respect for each other. When she's sleeping or studying, if you must have the TV on, be sure to turn it on a very low volume. When you want a little privacy, let her know in advance or work out a system or code to put on the door to let her know. When you do have a mini brawl, forgive quickly. If you make it through the first semester but you realize you and your roommate are opposites and her lifestyle is affecting you, put in a request to switch rooms ASAP. If it is really not working, you will have no regrets about the decision you made. You will be much happier and feel safer in the end.

**Side Note #11: Lock up everything valuable,** like your laptop, just in case there's a sleep walker on your floor who ends up in your room one night.

**Side Note #12—Since we're on the topic of computers:** You are going to have about two computers during your college term. One computer usually does not last the entire four years. It could be wear and tear or something like a virus that damages your hard drive and is irreparable. My computer died during my junior year and there was no way to retrieve the lost data. I was devastated. All my work for the past three years was gone. From this tragic occurrence, I learned to always back up my work by e-mailing the attachment to myself or using an external drive, like a flash drive, to save my important documents. Always be conscious of who is sending you files. Many viruses that are spread between you and your peers are passed on unintentionally. You can have a virus on your computer for quite some time before you realize that you have it. Purchasing antivirus software is well worth it. Many schools have free downloadable antivirus software, so be sure to take advantage of that as well. Again, be careful of leaving your laptop in locations such as the library and coffee shop without it being locked up. Laptops are items that are stolen on a frequent basis.

**Laptop or desktop?** It's really your call. A laptop is very convenient and mobile. You can take it anywhere you want to go. On the downside, it is more expensive than a desktop. Although a desktop is immobile, it usually lasts longer and is cheaper. If you can't afford a computer, there are plenty of computer labs on college campuses and some are even open for 24 hours that you can take full advantage of.

**Side Note #13:** Try to call your roommate before school begins and discuss the items you are bringing to avoid doubling up on some things that you don't need to have two or even three of. For example, you can bring the microwave and she can bring the blender. You will over pack the first time you move in, but you will learn in future semesters that you don't have to bring every single thing with you to college. There are many items I think you should have of your own, like utensils and a television. If your roommate has guests over and they are all using your utensils and you are sharing utensils, what are you going to use? If you have a favorite television program that comes on every Sunday at eight p.m. and so does she and you are sharing a TV, what show do you watch? If you can afford to, just have your own.

7. **Decorate your room**. It makes a world of difference. Now if you are a pretty plain person, you should still add features to the room that make it scream *you* all over. It will make your room much more cozy and inviting. Add a rug if there are bare floors. You do not have to go overboard in the first week with decorating. Slowly but surely your room will develop its own personality. In time, you'll get all types of school memorabilia that will really add definition to the room. Go wild with adding pictures of family members and friends.

Side Note #14: Every university is different, but if the university charges you for off-campus calls you make from your room phone, use your cell phone for all off-campus and long distance calls. Your cell phone usually has free night and weekend calls anyway. Do this and you just saved yourself a bill. (You still have to watch your cell phone's daytime minutes.)

Side Note #15: Be sure to have a sturdy pair of flip flops for the community showers!

8. **Walk straight past the credit card people who will try to coerce you into signing up for a credit card just for a free T-shirt.** It is not worth it! I would say one card is okay, but no card is probably best. Without self-control and with random expenses popping up, you can get into debt quite rapidly. The concept of a FICO score (credit score) may seem foreign to you and the least of your worries right now, but it will be important later on when you want to buy a car or get an apartment. Your credit history is very important. Credit card debt is not worth it. Something like student loan debt is worth it because you will eventually make a financial return on your academic investment once you graduate and get a job.

If you do get a credit card, make it a well thought out process. Compare interest rates, spending limits, and penalties for late payments of several companies. Don't just sign up for a bunch of credit cards for whatever prize they are offering.

> **Side Note #16:** Open up a bank account with the branch you have at home and at school so that your parents can deposit funds and you can easily access them on campus and forgo ATM charges. This may seem minor, but one dollar here, two dollars there in ATM fees add up. And when you are in college, that amount is even more significant. And why should you be charged for your own money anyway?

Now some of these golden rules may *not* be applicable to all students, especially if you are a commuter student or attending certain junior or community colleges. I wish that every school had on-campus housing and every student could live on campus at least their first year. There are so many perks, such as having close accessibility to campus resources and facilities. If the school is not structured for on-campus living or money issues force you to live at home, you will be perfectly fine. I would still advise you to attend the "getting to know you" sessions and make friends with students that actually live on campus. It may become useful when you want somewhere to sleep in-between classes or need to get a free meal of two off your friend's meal plan, and you can get the campus feeling without having to actually spend the money.

**Side Note #17:** Freshman year is one of the best years in college. Have fun!

# So what did you learn about the first days?

- Beat the rush.
- Attend as many freshmen "getting to know you/ ice breaker/team builder/floor meetings" as you can.
- Beware of dangerous groups that appear overly inviting and aggressive.
- Talk to an upperclassman about your schedule.
- Keep your eyes open and inquire about a good local hair salon.
- Buy your books used!
- Get an academic calendar.
- Get to know your roommate and *compromise.*
- Lock up everything valuable.
- Back up all your important documents.
- Walk around and see where your classes are generally located.
- Explore the surrounding town.
- Use your cell phone for off-campus and long distance calls if the university charges you.
- Decorate your room.
- Walk straight past the credit card people.
- Open up a bank account with the branch on campus to forgo ATM charges.
- Come in with a very open mind about your roommate.
- If you and your roommate have serious lifestyle differences and you have really tried to compromise, consider switching rooms for the following semester.

# TIP #1: HAVE FUN

For a portion of girls, this will be the very last time you have ultimate freedom of choice. You have the option to sleep in late, spend your day at the mall, stay in bed, or sit on a campus bench and feed the birds. There are a million things to do after your classes are over for the day or on the days you have no classes at all. What a life you have right now! You can believe in some of the most outrageous things and you will have twelve or so other students on campus that not only believe in the exact same thing, but are also ready to rally behind you to form a student group to combat the issue. Take advantage of this freedom (within limits).

Now is the time to bask in the fun that the campus has to offer! Join social clubs and common interest groups like Habitat for Humanity (you would be surprised how much fun community service can be). If you played sports in high school, join an intramural team. Whatever's your forte, girl, just do it!

**Transform yourself and explore your identity.** You may become a vegetarian one week, cut your hair off and go natural the following week, and then get a relaxer three months later. You have time to figure out what works for you and what doesn't. For your family's sake, don't go overboard and do any permanent damage, but do some of the things you always wanted to do, even if it's just for a semester. You are a work in progress and always under construction, at least for these next few years.

Watch your favorite shows with your dorm or apartment mates. Go on the school sponsored bus for freshmen to one of the clubs or parties in the area. Go ice or roller skating. Attend a lecture series sponsored by a cultural group. Go to a tailgate party, or attend the celebration after your college football team wins the game. Be spontaneous. **Do whatever you like to do, and have fun doing it!** You will have tons of unique and crazy escapades to reflect on one day with your friends. Make sure you take pictures to capture these moments.

Do something you would have never imagined yourself doing like going on a camping trip sponsored by the campus recreation center, attending a wine tasting event, or going wall climbing with a few friends. Take advantage of the (free) pool tables, movie theatre, bowling alley, or game room that your student fees are paying for. Dorms are nonstop entertainment, so leave you room door open so you don't miss out on all the fun going on in the hallway.

Go on spring break to fun and exotic places like Jamaica, Miami, or Cancun. Attend the love auctions for Valentine's Day, monthly poetry readings, or something out of your natural element, like an event sponsored by a cultural group you are unfamiliar with. Go to free lectures to hear renowned speakers. Attend a play. Go to the talent, comedy, or step show. Lounge in the local coffee shop for a while and read a good (non-school related) book. Go to a school-sponsored concert. Have fun chilling outside your room with the people on your floor. Go outside on a sunny day and play frisbee with your friends. On a snow day when campus is closed, have a snow ball fight or make a snow man.

Attend the football and basketball games and watch the halftime show. Attend homecoming events and go on the annual trip sponsored by an organization you are a member of. Eat in the dining hall with your friends and crack jokes on each other the entire time. Go to a student union party or fraternity party (but bring a friend or two along with you). Go out to eat. Go to happy hour or wing night at a local restaurant.

Join a dance group or become a fitness instructor at the gym. Talk until the sun comes up to one of your friends in one of those cushy seats in her room. Sit on a bench outside and people-watch. Play games, listen to music, and *laugh*! Attend events outside your campus in the local community or nearby universities. Enjoy life and don't be too serious all the time.

But, in the midst of all the fun you are having, the one very important thing you must keep in mind is to **do all your schoolwork first and have fun second.** When I started college, I was under the impression that college was a non-stop party. Fun, fun, FUN! Your friends will convince you to attend a party you know you should not attend because you have an exam the next day. They will swear that this is the party of the year. It is *never* the party of the year. What you'll realize quickly is that there is a lot of coursework that needs to be done amidst all of the fun you are having. Some of you may have grown up in a home where you had many restrictions placed on you and are now taking the opportunity to go wild. If you are having too much fun but not doing all of your work, there will be dire consequences. Don't let your desire for fun ruin you academically. Don't change your major from engineering to partying. You have to develop the discipline to foresee how a decision you make now can negatively impact you in the future. Learn this lesson early on in your college career and you will be well on your way to success!

## So what did you learn about having fun?

- Do whatever you like to do, try something you never thought you would, and have fun!
- Transform yourself. Explore your identity.
- Most important: Do your schoolwork first and have fun second.

# Tip #2: Maintain a High GPA (from the start)

**The most important semester of your college career is the first semester of your freshman year.** This semester has the most impact on your overall grade point average (GPA). You must work as hard as you can to get a 4.0 (all As)! This goal is within your reach. This will serve as a gauge for you to determine if you need to alter your study technique during future semesters. If you get a 4.0 or really close, your study plan worked. If you didn't even come close, it is time to alter your plan. You must study daily! Keep in mind that if you have classes Monday, Wednesday, and Friday, Tuesday and Thursday are not free days. Those days are meant to be study days.

Before I continue, let me define GPA. A semester GPA is simply the average grades earned during a specific semester. A cumulative GPA is the average of all of your grades earned during your entire enrollment in college. To calculate your GPA, you must take the value you receive in a class (A=4, B=3, C=2, D=1, F=0) and multiply it by the amount of credits the class is worth. Do this for every class you are taking for the semester. Add all of the total points you computed for each class and then divide that number by the total number of credit hours earned. Credit hours represent the number of hours you are in class for a week. So if a class is three credits, that usually means you are in class for three hours per week. Classes that involve labs are usually more credit hours because the lab component requires an extra hour or so of class time.

Once you do the above computation, this numerical value represents your semester GPA. Keep in mind, if your school uses the plus (+) and minus (-) system, those grades have different numerical values as well. For example, an A- is worth 3.7 points and a B+ is worth 3.3 points.

Let's look at an example of how to compute your GPA:

| Grade | Value | Credits | Total Points (value X credits) |
|-------|-------|---------|-------------------------------|
| A | 4 | 3 | 12 |
| A | 4 | 3 | 12 |
| B | 3 | 3 | 9 |
| B | 3 | 3 | 9 |
| C | 2 | 3 | 6 |
| Total | | 15 | 48 |

**GPA Computation:**

**Total Points (48) ÷ Total Credit Hours (15) = 48/15 = 3.2**

If you are currently a freshman, no matter how difficult your classes are now, there are much more difficult classes to come in future semesters. If you are a sophomore or above, no matter what happened freshman year, each semester gives you a new opportunity to start the semester off with an almost clean slate. You have the capability of improving your cumulative GPA. **During the beginning of every semester, from your freshman to senior years, you should commit to starting off in the right direction by putting in quality study time.**

If freshman year is over for you, you don't have as much GPA leverage, but good grades from now on will still have a significant impact in raising your GPA. Great grades in the beginning of each semester will make it easier at the end of the semester to get an A in the class. Professors take your first performance on an exam as an indication of how you are as a student. This will make professors more inclined to allow you to retake a test you performed poorly on the first time. Doing well academically from the start will not only make you stand out among your peers, but it will also make college so much more enjoyable.

**It is very difficult to try to raise a low GPA.** One low grade, like a C, D, or F, will make your GPA plummet downward substantially, while getting an A to raise a low GPA will not necessarily raise your GPA up to a desired level. (Later on I'll show you an example of how this happens.) Let your main focus be on achieving a high GPA during your first semester. Aim to begin with success. The more credit hours you have, the less GPA leverage there is, meaning even with good grades, the less your GPA moves in a positive direction.

**Side Note #1:** Keep in mind, if you are at school on an academic scholarship, you *can and will* lose your scholarship if you do not maintain a high GPA.

I am aware that many people may give you the "GPA isn't everything" speech, and although it may not be everything, it is *something*, particularly if it is really high or really low. A really high GPA says you are a hard worker, serious about your studies, have great time management skills, and a bunch of other positive qualities, including proof that you have actually *mastered* the subject at a college level (and that's exactly what employers and graduate schools want to see). A bad GPA says the opposite.

**Side Note #2:** Mastering the subject now will have a great impact on your *competence* in understanding the concepts to successfully complete the work assigned to you during jobs and internships, which will directly impact your *confidence* in your chosen profession.

Poor freshman-year grades prevent many people from getting into a great graduate school or graduating with honors. Your GPA is often the ticket to get you the interview for a job, being in the candidate pool for a scholarship, getting an internship, or being able to study abroad.

When an employer, recruiter, or admissions counselor looks at one hundred resumes, one way to narrow down the playing field is to say, "Let's only look at the resumes where the candidate has a GPA of 3.5 or above." The next step for the recruiter might be, "Let's look at their extracurricular activities and internship experience." This narrows down the playing field even more. When a recruiter looks at your resume with a 2.9 GPA, they may not know how fabulous and smart you are, or that you went through a particularly difficult experience second semester that lowered your GPA drastically. That's why you must **keep your GPA as high as possible as a buffer in case you do have a challenging semester or two later on.** You will be amazed at how your hard work translates into opportunities that are not available to everyone.

I'll use a simple GPA example. Let's pretend there are two freshman students: Student A and Student B. Let's look at both of their freshman year grades.

**Fall Freshman Year**

| | | Student A | Student B |
|---|---|---|---|
| AASP100 | Intro to AfroAm Study | A | B |
| COMM104 | Principle of Communication | A | B |
| Math116 | Calculus | B | C |
| NFSC101 | Elements of Nutrition | B | C |
| PHIL142 | Philosophy | A | B |
| | | | |
| Semester GPA | | 3.6 | 2.6 |
| Cumulative GPA | | 3.6 | 2.6 |

| Spring Freshman Year | | Both students received the same grades 2nd semester | |
| --- | --- | --- | --- |
| | | Student A | Student B |
| ECON250 | Intro to Micro Econ | A | A |
| BIO160 | Intro to Biology | A | A |
| ENGL101 | Freshman Engl | B | B |
| HIST145 | American Hist | B | B |
| CHEM120 | Organic Chem | C | C |
| | | | |
| Semester GPA | | 3.2 | 3.2 |
| Cumulative GPA | | 3.4 | 2.9 |

Based on the illustration you can see that Student A got off to a pretty good start. Student B did not. They both received the same grades the second semester and Student A still has a GPA above a 3.0 (where you definitely need to be) and Student B is hovering slightly below the 3.0 mark. The next question you probably have is, how do you maintain a high GPA from the start? There is no clear-cut formula. It depends on your familiarity with the subject, ability to comprehend the material, the professor, the time of day, and tons of other factors. But there is one thing that is universal for maintaining a high GPA and that's *studying*! Studying is the only guarantee that you will be adequately prepared for exams and quizzes that ultimately determine your grade in the class. Studying is covered in more detail in Tip #3: Study Daily. Raising a low GPA becomes more difficult with the more credits you have. The more credit hours you have, the less your cumulative GPA rises with an A in a particular class. And at that point the classes are so much harder. Study now and your hard work will pay off.

**If you are not doing well in a course, visit the professor and talk to them about the difficulties that you are having.** Really get to know your professors and teacher's assistants (TA's) very well, especially the person responsible for determining your final grade. If your professor knows you are trying, they may not fail you despite your performance. They may also have advice or other resources you can use that might not be public information. They may even tell you to visit them on a regular basis.

If your professors are a little standoffish at first, don't despair. You need a good grade in the class. Ask them about their career path or for advice based on their experiences. People love talking about themselves and this may soften them up a bit. Learn to adapt to their personality.

**Side Note #3:** You may need recommendations one day for a scholarship or graduate school, so building relationships with professors and making sure they know your name will put you in a perfect position later on.

**If your GPA is already very low, get on your grind and raise your GPA!** You have to get to work and show what you're made of! You can do it! This will be a great story for you to use later on when interviewing for jobs and internships. You can tell an interviewer how transitioning from high school was initially a challenge, but you figured out your areas of greatest weakness, quickly reassessed your study techniques and the actual time you were allocating to your studies, and have thrived as a result. You have received a 3.75–4.0 each semester thereafter. Interviewers love when you take proactive steps to improve your academic situation.

**Side Note #4:** Take the time to review a few resume sites that show examples of resumes that include your major GPA on your resume. This means you are showing the GPA in your major required classes, not the generic classes everyone has to take. Most of your major related classes are during your junior and senior years. Try your best in those classes and then average them out to compute your major GPA. Put your major GPA on your resume only if it is higher than your cumulative GPA. A last option is to exclude your GPA from your resume all together. Keep in mind, recruiters may still ask you for your GPA.

**Side Note #5:** There are many GPA calculating tools on the Internet. You can plug in your current grades and see what grades are needed for your remaining semesters to get your GPA to a desired level. Try any search engine and type in "GPA calculator."

## Additional Tips:

**1. Read Tip #3 and study daily!**

**2. Do your homework and keep up with reading and assignments.** (That has not changed.) If it is a problem set or a great amount of reading, break it up into smaller, more manageable pieces. Staying current with your assignments will allow you to get much more out of the lecture than if you are behind. Keep everything organized and assignments written down.

**3. Refer to your syllabus often throughout the semester.** Most importantly, when you first get your syllabus, read it in its entirety and highlight important points. Write down additional things your professor mentions that are not on the syllabus. Also, know how your final grade is calculated. Always be conscious of where you stand in the class and what you'll need on the final exam to maintain your grade or give you that extra boost to put you over the edge if you are right on the A-/B+ borderline.

**4. When choosing your classes for the semester, balance out your classes so that you do not have more than three difficult classes at one time.** Also, try not to take more than five classes a semester (fifteen credit hours), particularly during your freshmen year.

**5. Go to class (and exams) on time, perhaps even five minutes early.** Some classes may seem pointless to attend, but attend them. You may not realize you are getting anything from the lecture, but you are. Listening to the lecture, explanations to the homework assignment, and the professor's answers to classroom questions really bridges the information together in more ways than you think. Plus, if your classes aren't in huge lecture halls, your professors will notice that you attend class everyday.

They even notice the excessively tardy students. You want to get on your professor's good side, especially if you need help, want to negotiate a grade, or request a recommendation in the future. Also, be sure to go up to the professor at the end of class for clarification on any material you maybe having difficulty understanding.

**6. Visit each professor during their office hours several times throughout the semester** to get additional help on topics you do not understand. Come prepared with a list of questions.

**7. Take good notes.** Also, actively listen to what your professor is saying, meaning you are listening to the words coming out of your professor's mouth while simultaneously trying to process and interpret the information they are providing.

**8. Allow yourself only a few missed classes a semester.** Try to miss classes only for emergency situations.

**9. Sit in the front of the class.**

**10. Know the drop/add date!** If the class is not the right fit, drop it and add another course.

**11. Know the withdrawal date for classes!** If before the withdrawal date you have a D or F average, seriously consider withdrawing from the class! See if you can save the semester by talking to the professor. Know how many W's (withdrawals) you are allowed to have on your transcript.

I want you to realize that if it is a required course, you will still have to take this course during another semester and most students do not have the time in their schedule to take a W more than once or twice. W's on your transcript are better than F's but they are still unfavorable, so consider when you are willing to receive a W. It would probably be best if you take a W in an upper level course (courses during your junior and senior year) that will be much more difficult than a freshman year course.

**12. During your junior and senior year when you want to take a course to improve an area you may be weak in, see if you can take the class pass/fail so that it does not factor into your GPA.**

**13. Take challenging courses at a community college during the summer, but only take classes unrelated to your major.** For example, if you are a marketing major, take all your marketing courses at your main university, but take a class like calculus at a community college. Calculus is a more challenging course, and it is not a major marketing class. Any course with the word "marketing" in it should be taken at your major college, not a community college. I took my intro accounting course at a community college and got an A. Accounting 101 is a foundations course, so I should have taken it at my university. I took the rest of my accounting curriculum at my university and found that the community college course wasn't nearly as detailed or challenging as the courses at my university. This may vary depending on the caliber of your community college, but my recommendation is that when it comes to your major, take the best classes you possibly can.

**Side Note #6:** Taking summer courses also enables you to finish school faster and at a lower cost. Just make sure the credit hours transfer over to your main college. Check with your advisor about the paperwork you may have to fill out.

**14. Turn your assignments in on time.**

**15. Always get the full class participation points.** There is absolutely no reason why you should not get full credit for participation. Participate every day in each class. Overcome your shyness and refuse to be invisible. Try to focus on the grade you want to achieve in the course. Read the night before or a couple of nights before class and jot down a few notes. Make a commitment to yourself to participate daily in each class. Also, never be afraid to raise your hand and ask questions if you need clarity.

**16. *Always* do extra credit.** These are points that raise your GPA and usually require minimal work to attain. If you are a few percentage points shy from the next grade up, extra credit can give you an A- instead of a B+.

**17. Look into acquiring old exams** from students that took the course the previous semester or see if your school provides a test center that sells old exams released from professors. Prepare for the exam by redoing old exam questions. You will probably have similar questions on your exam.

**18. Use all the time allotted for exams.** This is one of those situations where it does not pay to be a speed demon. Also, don't spend too much time on one question. Use any extra time to review your answers. Usually the first choice you make is the correct choice, so unless you're sure, don't change your answers just for the fun of it.

**19. Go to the writing center and other resources** on campus where graduate students edit your papers. Some professors give extra points on a paper for utilizing these resources.

> **Side Note #7:** Learn to type at a fast speed. This will help you complete papers faster. Also, enhance your technological skills beyond a basic word processing program like Microsoft Word. Depending on your major, you may have to know other specific technological skills, so know them! Do not leave college without becoming computer literate. Employers will expect this of you.

**20. Learn if your school has a "class repeat" option,** where you can retake a class if you failed the first time around during your freshman year, and the old grade is erased from your transcript.

**21. Know your weak areas and get all the help that you need through on-campus resources,** like a math tutorial program.

**22. When turning in a paper, presentation means a lot.** Make sure your paper is free of grammatical errors, typed, spaced properly, the correct font, and *error free*. **Use spell check!** You may want to add a report cover to give it an extra boost. Send it to your parents or an older sibling for a quick edit before submitting it to your professor. Also, always read your written work out loud to yourself to identify errors you may have missed. A written paper is meant to go through several drafts until you end up with a final product. If a teacher tells you to submit a rough draft for them to review, *never* turn in an actual rough draft. Turn in your best product as your rough draft. Also, on exams that have a written component, be as neat as possible. When professors are grading a million exams, they have limited tolerance trying to decipher your hieroglyphics.

**23. Work to get along with different personalities during group projects/presentations:** Most people hate group projects, but all students have to do them. This is an attempt by the university to prepare you for the "real world" where you will have to juggle different personalities and still get a remarkable end product. Try to keep the end in mind. Do not get caught up trying to control difficult team members. Do your part and do it well. Keep in mind that if there are slackers in the group, you might have to help pick up their slack, but do what you must because your name is attached to that final grade.

**24. Argue your grade if you have to,** in a polite yet assertive manner. Never become rude and abrasive to authority. An unfavorable approach doesn't increase your chances of getting a grade change in the course. Do you think you really deserved an A instead of a B? You should be very honest with yourself. If you really deserve partial credit, see if you can get your grade changed. There's a great chance that your request will be dismissed, but it's worth a try if you have good supporting evidence. Make sure to check your semester grades frequently after the semester is over to give yourself ample time to talk to the professor about your grade change before everyone leaves campus.

# So what did you learn about maintaining your GPA?

- The most important semester of your college career is the first semester of your freshman year.
- During the beginning of every semester, from your freshman to senior years, start the semester off in the right direction by putting in quality study time.
- Doing well academically from the start will not only make you stand out among your peers, it also makes college much more enjoyable.
- It is very difficult to try to raise a low GPA.
- Although your GPA may not be everything, it is something—particularly if it is really high or really low.
- Keep your GPA as high as possible as a buffer in case you do have a challenging semester or two later on.
- Maintain a high GPA by *studying daily*! Re-read tip #3.
- If you are not doing well in a course, visit the professor and talk to him or her about the difficulty you are having.
- If your GPA is already very low, get on your grind and raise your GPA!
- Do your homework and keep up with reading and assignments.
- Refer to your syllabus often throughout the semester.

- When choosing your classes for the semester, have no more than three difficult classes in one semester. Also, try not to take more than five classes a semester (fifteen credit hours) particularly during your freshman year.
- Go to class (and exams) on time.
- Visit each professor in their office hours several times throughout the semester.
- Take good notes.
- Allow yourself only a few missed classes a semester.
- Sit in the front of the class.
- Know the drop/add date!
- Know the withdrawal date for classes!
- During your junior and senior year when you want to take a course to improve an area in which you may be weak, see if you can take the class pass/fail.
- Take challenging courses at a community college during the summer, but only take classes *unrelated* to your major.
- Turn your assignments in on time.
- Always get the full class participation points.
- *Always* do extra credit.
- Look into acquiring old exams.
- Use all the time allotted for exams.
- Go to the writing center.
- Learn if your school has a "class repeat" option.
- Know your weak areas and get all the help that you need through on-campus resources.

- When turning in a paper, remember that presentation means a lot.
- Work to get along with different personalities during group projects/presentations.
- Argue your grade (in a polite manner) if you have to.

# Tip #3: Study Daily

You should **allocate several hours in the day for focused study.** It may seem like a lot, but the amount of focused study time you devote to your day will have a direct positive impact on the grades you receive, if you study efficiently. Efficient studying is actual study time, which includes reading, highlighting, note-taking, etc. This does not include chit-chatting with others in the library or surfing the Internet.

Most books on effective study techniques will tell you to read your notes right after class. By the time you are finished with class, you are so excited to get out of there and catch a quick nap before your next class begins that the last thing you are thinking about doing is skimming your notes. You should, however, develop the discipline to do this. **Take good notes while in class and review your notes right after class.** Good notes will be a huge help when it comes time to prepare for your exams.

It is recommended that you triple your study time in proportion to your in-class time. If you have five classes, that's fifteen hours a day. Realistically, there really aren't enough hours in the day to reach that goal. So **you do have to incorporate weekends into your study plan.** As much as you would love to use weekends to sleep and have fun, you have to put in a bit of studying. Some people need less study time, while others need more. The amount of studying you allocate to your day also varies depending on the subject and the professor. **Five to seven hours daily is a good benchmark to begin with.**

You'll soon discover that every professor believes that his or her class is the only class you're taking and will assign massive amounts of work, as if you have no other coursework for the semester. So test it out and see the amount of time that is appropriate for you to devote to studying. More focused study is *always* better than less, but this does not mean you should be studying every hour of the day. Now if you notice that you *always* have a great deal of free time, then you should be studying more.

For those who struggled to have decent grades in high school, although you were not an A student then, that does not mean you cannot be an A student in college. A's are not necessarily given to the smartest student. A's are given to the student who is the most consistent in their focused study in preparation for the things that count toward the final grade, such as exams, midterms, and finals. **The best way to be prepared is to stay current with your studies.** Create a study plan. Divide your subjects and create goals you want to achieve during your study time frame. For example, a goal for a biology class could be to read chapter five and take notes within two and a half hours.

**Side Note #1: Not everyone comes to college equipped with the best study strategies, so no, you are not weird.** College does require much more independent study. If you came into college with proven effective study habits, you have a *great* advantage over your peers. In high school, studying was never as intense. As a matter of fact, a lot of people did not study in high school at all. You typically saw the same teachers every day, so the information was always fresh in your mind. In college, you may have a class once or twice a week and may not have any homework at all. This can make tests extremely difficult. This is why you must take responsibility for your success in each class by studying daily. Exams sneak up on you.

**Side Note #2:** You could have been *the* girl in high school: straight A's, always on the high honor roll, ranked in the top twenty-five of your class, and captain of just about everything. You may have even come into college with a number of advanced placement credits. It is still important to remember that **college is not the same as**

**high school and you have to be on top of your studying to get and maintain a high GPA.**

Choosing where you study and the time of day is up to you. Some people are night owls, while some are early birds. You should know the time of the day that is best for you to study. Some people love the library or computer lab, while others prefer to stay in their room. Wherever you go, make sure it is comfortable, well lit, and free from distractions.

I learned early in college that when I studied in my room, my bed would actually call out my name. It would say, "Sheryl, come lie down. It's just a five minute power nap." And before I knew it, it would be the following morning. I'd lie to myself and say, "Oh I'll just wake up at five a.m. and finish this paper." When work and sleep are your two options, sleep always seems to win. If you also have a talking bed, *leave your room*! **Never study in your bed.** Do your work first and sleep later. There is a slim to nonexistent chance you will actually wake up when you plan to. If you do actually wake up and work on your paper, there is a strong chance that the quality of your paper will suffer tremendously.

**You should study during the free moments you have every day, such as the time in between classes.** This breaks up the required hours of study into smaller, more manageable timeframes.

If you know how to do every single homework assignment, class, and review problem, as well as old quizzes, and exams without looking at the answer for assistance, you should be ready for the exam. This will give you a good idea that you know everything that the professor could possibly present on the exam. A similar approach should be taken for classes that are not quantitative (i.e. a literature course). Know all the information that could possibly be asked. Take notes and identify themes in the text so that if an essay question is asked, you have strong examples from which to draw answers from.

**Side Note #3:** Always set your alarm clock (or maybe even your cell phone alarm as well) to ensure that you do not oversleep on exam day.

Let me reiterate this point: You should study *daily*. Attend the review sessions provided by your professor and be able to answer all of the homework assignment, in-class, and review questions on your own before the exam. Don't believe those who claim to always cram for exams and somehow pass. Either they are lying or can risk not studying. **Laziness, procrastination, and lack of studying are three deadly sins.** You have too much at stake and a future that is too bright to take that risk. So remember, consistent daily study is the key to success!

## Additional Tips:

**1. Buy a book on study techniques for college students or take a 0-1 credit course designed to teach freshmen study skills.**

**2. Get into a study routine as soon as possible. Try to figure out the techniques that work for you and those that do not.** Is it highlighting the text? Making flashcards? Rereading the text three times? A combo of all three? I had a friend whose tactic was to read the text once while taking her own notes. Once she went through all of the material, she reread her notes several times, and it worked like a charm every time. I had another friend who reread the text three times and that worked for her as well. Others I knew rewrote their lecture notes and that worked for them. You have to figure out what works for you.

> **Side Note #4:** Often times interruptions while you are studying are unavoidable, but commit to not checking your e-mail, watching television, or surfing the net while studying.

**3. Read and reread your notes and text, and perhaps even rewrite your lecture notes.**

**4. During an extended study session, study the more difficult subject first while you are the most alert.**

**5. Master materials thoroughly before your exams and prep well in advance (one to two weeks prior).**

**6. Attend class** (oh yes, this again). Teachers love to tell bonus information for the exam to students who actually attend class.

**7. Pay attention in class and try to "get it" the first time.** Try to learn the day's lecture that day so that by the time the examination is given, it will be more like a review and not as though you are learning the information for the very first time.

**8. During long study sessions, take breaks every hour.**

**9. Limit your daily TV intake to free up more time for studying.**

**10. Participate in study groups.** I *strongly* believe this a great study mechanism that is often underutilized. Group study does not mean socializing time (but of course it will happen sometimes). It means doing independent study on your own and them coming together as a group to learn from each other. This group should not be one in which you are vastly the strongest group member. Include at least one person who you think has a stronger understanding of the material than you. You don't want this to turn into you becoming the teacher the entire night, (although this does strengthen your retention of the material). If you need to strengthen a specific area, make sure you get the help you need first, and then teach others second.

**11. Don't be fooled by open book exams.** Students hear "open book" and think that means they do not have to study. Open book exams usually only work to your advantage if you are up to date in the class. You should still study the material and have a general idea of where things are located within the text so that you do not waste time by flipping through your textbook to find information.

**12. For math exams, make sure you have committed the formulas you need to memory and do a thorough job of checking your answers on exams. For essay questions on exams, write down key points you are going to use to formulate your response**. This ensures that you actually answer the essay question and don't go off on a tangent. If you are totally lost and confused by an essay response, try to write down all you know related to the topic and pray for partial credit. Just don't leave it blank.

**13. Avoid cramming (but if desperate, pull an all-nighter).** Before my junior year I thought, *What?! Me? All night with no sleep? Not happening.* During my junior year I came to realize that all-nighters were sometimes worth it. Grab your caffeinated drink and review the material for the exam the next day. You can forgo a little bit of sleep for a decent grade. If you are cramming, you probably cannot learn *all* the material in one night, but it's better than not studying at all. At least if it's multiple choice, you stand a good chance of passing. Try to limit cramming for emergency situations only. Go to the library or twenty-four-hour computer lab and study away. With less sleep before the exam, you have to be careful not to oversleep for your exam. Do remember that consistent daily study is always better than cramming.

**14. Divide large amounts of reading material into smaller, more manageable pieces.**

**15. Squeeze in study time by reading while on the elliptical trainer at the gym or carry flashcards in your purse to review notes while waiting in the doctor's office.**

**16. Get a friend in each class to take notes for you when you're absent.** Get all their contact information and offer this service to them as well for days they are absent.

> **Side Note #5:** If you have a learning disability, visit your school's disability support center. You may be able to take exams in the center and be given extended time to complete exams. There was a girl in one of my classes with a learning disability and she arranged for someone in class to share their notes with her. Go to the center and see the options that are available for you to be successful.

# So what did you learn about studying daily?

- Take good notes while in class and review your notes right after class.
- Allocate several hours in the day for focused study and incorporate weekends into your study plan.
- Five to seven hours daily is a good benchmark to begin with, for the hours of required study.
- The best way to be prepared for exams is to stay current with your studies.
- Not everyone comes to college equipped with the best study strategies.
- College is not the same as high school and you have to be on top of your studying to get and maintain a high GPA.
- If you have a talking bed that calls out your name when you study in your room, *leave your room*!
- You should study during the free moments you have every day.
- Laziness, procrastination, and lack of studying are three deadly sins.
- Buy a book on study techniques for college students or take a 0-1 credit course designed to teach freshmen study skills.
- Get into a study routine as soon as possible. Try to figure out the techniques that work for you.
- Read and reread the notes and text, and perhaps even rewrite your lecture notes.
- Master materials thoroughly before your exams and prep well in advance (one to two weeks prior).

- During an extended study session, study the more difficult subjects first, while you are the most alert.
- Attend class, pay attention, and try to "get it" the first time.
- During extended study sessions, take breaks in between studying.
- Limit your daily TV intake to free up more time for studying.
- Participate in study groups!
- Don't be fooled by open book exams.
- Know the formulas for math exams. For essay questions, immediately jot down key points as an outline for writing your response.
- Avoid cramming (but if needed, pull an all-nighter).
- Divide large amounts of reading material into smaller, more manageable pieces.
- Squeeze in study time by reading while on the elliptical trainer at the gym or carry flashcards in your purse to review notes while waiting in the doctor's office.
- Get a friend in each class to take notes for you when you're absent.

# Tip #4: Choose the Right Major (for you)

There is an infamous phrase that says, "Do what you love and you will eventually make money from it." Most people would say this statement is true, *but* it should be interpreted with a disclaimer because it often does more harm than good. It often gives students a false sense of how much each individual must contribute to their own success. **Each student, regardless of major, has to take their future and career into their own hands.** There isn't a job or graduate school ready and waiting for you unless you take the necessary steps to make it happen. A college degree is no longer the job guarantee it used to be. **A degree is only as valuable as you make it.**

If you are a freshman right now and your major is undeclared, welcome to the club of freshman and sophomores across the country. There are thirty-something-year-olds still trying to figure out what they want to do with their lives. Some students have known since birth that they wanted to become a dentist; others decided while in college how much they love science and are willing to devote time now for an extremely rewarding career and lifestyle in the future. Choosing a major isn't as easy for everyone.

Does is it really matter what you major in? The answer is ambiguous. Yes, your major matters because college is the training ground for your future profession. If your goal is to be a journalist, it only makes sense that you major in journalism. You can also major in French, and still end up being a journalist. **In the end, your passion and drive is really what matters, but majoring in a particular subject and studying it in detail puts you in the best position to be successful in the field.** The same goes if you choose a particular major, graduate with a degree, and realize that you don't really enjoy the subject area anymore. No, you have not hit a brick wall or a dead end. Although it may not be easy, you can always change your career path.

You should analyze what you're good at (strengths), what you're not so good at (weaknesses), and what will keep you getting up in the morning (your passion). You should also factor in things such as job availability upon graduation and what's important to you: financial security, a job you love, upward mobility, etc. Safe majors are majors that lead to jobs in high-demand fields, like nursing, in which there will be tons of jobs available once you graduate; however, even in high-demand fields, you have to be stay on top of finding and securing a position. Also, a safe major still requires that you become the best at what you do. I chose a safe major, yet I still saw tons of my peers with the same "safe" major struggle to get internships and jobs. It goes back to your passion, drive, and willingness to put in the work and learn as quickly as you can from your mistakes.

It is the uncertain outcome of majors like Dance or Women's Studies why parents try to persuade their children to choose safe majors, where you are guaranteed a good job with a high salary and a bright path for advancement. The question people immediately ask once you tell them about your unsafe major is, "So what are you going to do with that?" Your parents don't want you to struggle to find a job after graduation. There are usually more job opportunities for students with safe majors, as well as job security and financial stability. Parents usually condone unsafe majors when it's not their money paying for the tuition (i.e. you have a full-time scholarship to major in it). They want you to have a more lucrative profession and life than they had. When you choose certain majors, parents fear that there may be fewer positions out there from which to choose. You may have to put in more work to create an opportunity for yourself, but the reward will be ten-fold when that opportunity does present itself if you are really passionate about the field.

At the end of the day, you, not your parents, will have to deal with your decision. Major in what interests and excites you, something that you will probably enjoy or will fit into the lifestyle you want for yourself. Follow your intuition. The choice you make will have to be your own. **Try to have a major in mind by the end of your freshman year, but no later than the end of your sophomore year, so you can begin to line up your internships as soon as possible.**

The reality for most black girls is that you and your family have spent or will spend an enormous amount of money funding college, but when you are out of school, you will be the one living with the decision, so do what you are enthusiastic about! Enthusiasm goes a long way when you are in school because you will be the person putting in the work studying the subject, not your parents. This enthusiasm will carry on after you graduate and begin working in the field.

If you like your major and profession, it won't seem as if are doing work and you'll probably do it well. Do consider the pros and cons of the major you choose and the advice of people you trust and care for you. There may be lots of hard work, sleepless nights, and some days of actually reconsidering your major that may be in store for you. English majors may have tons of papers; business majors may have to endure lots of lectures and group projects, but hang in there. **Everything in life takes work.**

> **Side Note #1:** When considering your major, do research to determine if obtaining a graduate degree such as your master's or PhD is typical within the profession. Don't let extra schooling ever dissuade you from a profession, such as medicine. You may need to factor in things like your ability to afford extra schooling, but remember that financial aid is out there. The rewards of many of these professions far outweigh the time you put in.

So yes, your major matters in many regards, particularly as it relates to immediate opportunities upon graduation. If you are a music major, becoming a professional musician may be difficult, as well as present concerns about financial stability. You may not be getting a paycheck every two weeks or have health insurance as many other professionals might have; however, if you are really talented and persevere, there is a possibility that you will go beyond your furthest expectation.

For example, let's look at a *successful* music major versus an *unsuccessful* music major. The *unsuccessful* music major would not put in any work, yet still have the expectation of success once they finished school. (A very false sense of entitlement!) The *successful* music major would hone her talent by practicing daily, seek out opportunities to perform, and persevere through setbacks and rejection. The *successful* music major would network with current musicians to understand some of the hurdles they faced. They too perhaps had to work at a job unrelated to their major to make sure their bills were paid. They may have had to pursue music on the side until an opportunity presented itself in which they could become a musician on a full-time basis. The *successful* music major realizes that anything unrelated to music is a means to an end and does not dictate the rest of one's life. The *successful* music major continues to audition and ends up having a lucky break and lives out her wildest dream of being a musician. Now of course this fairy tale does not happen to everyone, and that's the reality that needs to be factored in when making the decision about your major. What are some alternatives if things don't work out as planned? Become a music teacher? Composer? Think of all the successful musicians, actresses, and artists. They didn't all just start out on top.

The same story of perseverance and drive also applies to conventional or safe majors, like biology or chemistry majors who hope to become a doctor one day. Yes, being a doctor is a lucrative profession in many ways, but if you don't study daily, maintain a high GPA, obtain internships or research opportunities, and develop a winning resume and interview skills, you can end up not fulfilling your dream of becoming a doctor one day. Everyone has situations and circumstances that may impede them from moving forward, but maturity means doing a real self-assessment and realizing that you ultimately determine your own reality. **It is important that you stay on your grind before and after you graduate, no matter what your major is.**

If a particular major taps into your passion, be an expert in the field. Do it and do a really good job at it. Get your master's and PhD in it if you want to. Dream big and develop your God-given talents. **Just make sure that you are focused with whatever you decide to do.** You can have a rewarding career path with any major you choose. It is okay to start out with a major and switch it one, two, or three times, but it's important to keep in mind that that decision may cost you money in lost credits and additional time at the university. Now if you need to change your major, change it, because no matter the cost, it's definitely *not* worth continuing with a major you absolutely dislike.

After I graduated, I remember eavesdropping on a conversation a few freshmen girls were having about their major. One girl in particular stood out to me. Her major was pharmacy and I listened to her as she spoke about the difficulty she was having in her chemistry class and how she was ready to switch to an "easier" major. I really wanted to jump in on that conversation. There was probably a reason why this young lady chose pharmacy as her major. She was probably gifted in the sciences and had a real interest in pursuing this career path. Now that she had discovered it was a bit challenging, she wanted to give up. Now I'm not a science person, so if I were to make the mistake of majoring in the sciences, it would make sense for me to change my major, but it seemed from the conversation that she really wanted to be a pharmacist. It just seemed out of her reach. I wish I was able to show her the possibility of her life. There was so much success around the corner, but a few challenges blurred her vision.

Now, I am not saying that you should stick with something you absolutely hate, but an easier major is not necessarily the answer. The easy element to your major may limit your earning potential, availability of jobs, or general interest. Know that you can major in something you *like*, and pursue other things you *love* in your free time. You can also minor in it, double major (one degree and two majors), obtain a double degree (two degrees), use up your electives on classes related to that subject, or join clubs and organizations that are related to the subject.

I have realized along the way that **the things that are really worth knowing aren't necessarily the easiest things to master.** I was an accounting major. Accounting was not easy and I do not recommend that everyone become an accounting major. After researching the profession thoroughly, I had to do a little soul searching. What did I love doing? I loved writing. What was important to me? Traveling, making a difference, and shopping. What enormous expenses would I have coming out of school? Over $20,000 in student loan debt. So that ruled out being a full-time freelance writer. What were some of my other interests? Business. What is the language of business? Accounting. What are the perks to the profession that tie into some of my interests: travel, learning the ins and out of business, and an annual salary lucrative enough to pay off my student loans. Bingo! This process just seemed simple, but it took about three good years before I knew in my heart it was a good decision. On the days I wanted to change majors, I trusted my gut and my gut told me to stick with it. I could not see the end—me actually being an accountant and loving it, but I had to trust that I was moving in the right direction. Do I have to totally push aside my passion of writing? No, I can still write in my leisure, and who knows, one day I might throw that calculator out the window and become a full-time writer. My first job or profession out of college does not dictate how the rest of my life pans out.

During the summer before my senior year I was sick and went to see an ear, nose, and throat specialist. I thought I was going for a consultation, but I ended up getting some really valuable advice. He said, "Sheryl, do you think I *love* being an ear, nose, and throat specialist? I *like* it, but I don't *love* it. It is my profession. **Your profession does not have to define who you are as a person.** To succeed in any profession you must master the material. Society respects someone that masters their field and you will be well paid if you are the best at what you do. You just can't be all over the place." That piece of advice really made sense to me.

There are tradeoffs no matter the decision you eventually make, but if you work in an environment where you are unfulfilled, even if you make tons of money, that situation will be a drag. Some people are more service oriented, so Teach for America is a perfect option for them. A close friend of mine is an investment banker and works one hundred hours per week. She likes it and has a very lucrative salary. I have a friend that works less than forty hours per week as a teacher and makes a third of what my one hundred hour per week friend makes, but she loves it and is totally fulfilled. Any profession you choose will come with a tradeoff. For example, pediatricians have a great salary, but they have to put in many years of schooling and come out with thousands of dollars in student loan debt. Everything comes with a price tag. **Have the determination to put in the work.** There is no such thing as a free ride.

Once you have personally assessed your skill sets, you will probably notice a general theme that will point you to a particular career in specific areas such as the arts, business, the health professions, computer/technology areas, or perhaps more service oriented fields. Realize that you may go into one field and work there for a particular amount of time and then head in a totally opposite direction.

If you are like me, you love a little bit of everything, so it is understandable that many possible majors are floating through your head. Many freshmen and sophomores are under the impression that choosing a major is so dire that if you do not choose the right one, you will be stuck in a profession you hate for a long time. There are so many things out there that you may enjoy that narrowing it down to one thing seems nearly impossible. I was the same way. Every time I took a class I enjoyed, I thought that was where I should head professionally. So how did I finally make the decision?

**I befriended my advisor and met with her monthly.** Advisors may have a host of valuable information or they can be a total waste. It is usually one or the other. You should be in the advising office perhaps once a month or so and have a list of questions ready if you are confused at all about anything. That is what they are being paid to do. Scheduling can be near impossible at the beginning and end of the semester so you may have to wait a week or two before you actually get an appointment, but be patient.

I also took **the career assessment tests offered in the campus career center and several other assessments I found online.** This can usually help you to at least narrow down the field you seem to work well in, your skill sets, and patterns of interest. It will force you to assess your strengths, weaknesses, values, strongest subjects in school, and extra-curricular activities that were most enjoyable and can translate into a career. They have a bunch of diagnostic tests like Myers Briggs. My test told me to major in marketing, and although that didn't end up being my major, I still ended up pursuing a business degree, so at least that narrowed down my options. **You have to invest considerable time researching your career field of interest.** This includes the major, job options, internships offered, and particular courses you must complete or tests you must pass to be certified in your profession. Also investigate the enrollment process for that major at your particular university. It may be a limited enrollment program and highly competitive to get into, so only the top students that apply will actually be admitted into the program. The Internet is a great place to start. Your campus career center, library, and talking to individuals in the field are also valuable options.

**What Happens After I Choose a Major?**

**After you choose your major, immerse yourself fully in it.** Join organizations and run for a leadership position within the organization such as president, vice president, or treasurer of the club. Having a leadership position gives you direct exposure to employers when you have to set up meetings and company presentations. Talk to professors and alumni, read trade magazines and journals, go to conferences, get internships, research and stay abreast of current events and new pronouncements related to your profession. Thoroughly research the major at your school.

If you think you need to go to graduate school, be sure to attend the free campus lectures on preparing for whichever test you must pass to get into graduate school whether it be the GRE, GMAT, LSAT, or something else. You may want to consider taking a prep course for this exam during your junior year.

When researching your major, ask: *What are the GPA requirements to get into the honors program related to the major? What are the deadlines to apply? Will I have to write a senior thesis in the program? Are there any prerequisite courses I need to take to get in? What are the requirements to graduate with honors (cum laude, magna cum laude, or summa cum laude)? Do all students with a 3.5 graduate cum laude or is this calculation on a weighted basis?*

**Side Note #2:** Take all the classes you can possibly take that relate to your major to enhance your knowledge.

## What about Double Majoring?

There is really no requirement that you have to double major unless you want to (or have to, based on state or other licensing requirements). Majoring in something that complements another major, like international business and Spanish, can be value added; however, keep in mind that those majors alone (such as *just* being an international business major) can probably reap many of the same benefits, meaning you might end up with the same job as your peers who double majored. Do you have a leg up as a double major? Yes, maybe. You have mastered a foreign language that will make conducting business much more effective and efficient. What's the trade off? The student who double majored could have paid additional costs for summer classes or an extra semester at the university. When you factor in how much of an asset this student will be in a Spanish speaking setting, then it might be worth it. Another good reason to double major is if you have an abstract interest and you want to add this to a conventional major.

No matter what your major is, you must have an internship or two before your senior year. You should also try your best to secure your full-time job or acceptance into law/med or whatever graduate school you want to attend *before* you graduate. If you don't get into graduate school or get a job for after graduation, have a plan B in place. When you are in school, you have a plethora of recruiters seeking you out. The longer you are out of school without employment, the less attractive you become. If you are out of school for over a year without employment, the new graduating class will be ready and waiting to fill the new job slots that open up. Be smart about fully using the career development resources on campus so that you will be in the position to pick and choose where you want to work as opposed to having to take whatever you can get.

# So what did you learn about choosing the right major (for you)?

- Each student, regardless of major, has to take her future and career into her own hands.
- A degree is only as valuable as you make it.
- In the end, your passion and drive is really what matters, but majoring in a subject and studying it in detail puts you in the best position to be successful in that particular field.
- Try to have a major in mind by the end of your freshman year, but no later than the end of your sophomore year, so you can begin to line up your internships as soon as possible.
- Everything in life takes work.
- It is important that you stay on your grind before and after you graduate, no matter what your major is.
- Make sure that you are focused on whatever you are doing.
- The things that are really worth knowing aren't necessarily the easiest things to master.
- Have the ambition to put in the work. There is no such thing as something for nothing.
- Befriend your advisor and meet with him or her monthly.
- Take the career assessment tests offered in the campus career center. This can usually help you to at least narrow down the fields in which you seem to work well, your skill sets, and patterns of interest.

- You have to invest considerable time researching your career field of interest. This includes the major, job options, internships offered, and particular courses you must complete to be certified in your particular profession.

- When you choose your major, immerse yourself fully in it. Join organizations, run for a leadership position (this also gives you direct exposure to employers), read trade magazines and journals, go to conferences, get internships, research and stay current on events and new pronouncements related to your profession. Thoroughly research the major at your school.

- Double major if two majors complement each other or if you have another abstract interest.

- No matter what your major is, you must have an internship or two before your senior year. You should also try your best to secure your full-time job or acceptance into graduate school before you graduate.

# Tip #5: Get Involved Early On

When you first get to college, the magnitude of a college campus or even a lecture hall can be overwhelming. One way to make a large campus feel smaller is to get involved in clubs and organizations. The people you meet in these settings can become just like extended family members. Making connections with other students creates a sense of belonging at any university.

What you will receive from your involvement in clubs and organizations is invaluable. **The experience shapes your leadership, communication, networking, time management, and public speaking skills.** You will expand your network and have quality information to put on your resume that will help you to secure internships and jobs. You will also have fun in the process. Your involvement in extracurricular activities will probably be one of the highlights of your college experience.

With that said, let's look into some of the things you can get involved with. There is *so* much to do. Here are a few examples:

**1. Cultural Groups:** Cultural groups give you the opportunity to connect with students of a similar heritage and background. Some examples include the African Student Association, Black Student Union, and Caribbean Student Association. These groups can become very family oriented. Being involved in these organizations can make you feel as if you never left your native land or old neighborhood. There are certain mannerisms and jokes that people of the same nationality share. These organizations also sponsor events such as concerts, lectures, and fashion shows. A cultural group is a great way to connect with students similar to yourself.

**2. Service/Volunteer Activities:** I have always believed that to whom much is given, much is expected. Service activities are opportunities to get out in the community and give back. Examples include the Red Cross, Habitat for Humanity, or a homeless shelter.

**3. Sororities:** Sororities are opportunities to create strong relationships with like-minded women on issues that are important, such as community service, political issues, and attaining high academic goals. Research the organization's values, talk to members, and attend the events to decide which sorority, if any, is the right fit for you. Don't make plans to become a part of a sorority your freshman year, but begin to learn more about the organization.

## Historically Black Sororities

Alpha Kappa Alpha Sorority, Inc.

Delta Sigma Theta Sorority, Inc.

Sigma Gamma Rho Sorority, Inc.

Zeta Phi Beta Sorority, Inc.

**4. Academic Clubs:** These clubs are based on your major, like the Marketing or Pre-Dental Club. Being involved in a group like this looks great in the eyes of a recruiter. As mentioned in the last chapter on choosing a major, involvement in the organization affiliated with your major will expose you to many facets of the profession. These organizations will also provide networking opportunities that you probably would not get elsewhere. Involvement in these organizations is essential to your career success.

**5. Advocacy:** These groups are ones in which students fight for a cause. Some examples are the American Civil Liberties Union or an animal rights group. These groups are very passionate about their beliefs. If you have a strong belief, join an advocacy group! Just try not to get arrested or end up on the five o'clock news while fighting your cause.

**6. Governing Body/Political Groups:** If you plan to go to law school, want to run for an elected office, or just love government organizations, join a governing body or political group. Examples include the Student Government Association or Residence Hall Association. You can also join an organization like Young Democrats or Young Republicans.

**7. Honors:** If your grades are spectacular, like I am assuming they will be, many honor societies will send you a special request to become a member. There are other honors programs that you will have to apply to directly. If your grades allow you to qualify, join an honor society like Omicron Delta Kappa (ODK) or Phi Sigma Pi.

**8. Media:** If you want to know more about what is going on around campus, become involved in media outlets. Become a part of the campus newspaper, yearbook editorial staff, or become a part of your college radio station. If your school has a television station and students have an opportunity to work there, see how you can become involved.

**9. Performing:** If you took ballet for seven years of your childhood and would like to maintain your ability to do a dancer's split, join a dance troupe. If you want to tap into your inner actress, join an acting group or become a part of a play.

**10. Recreation:** Just for the fun of it or if you weren't able to go to college for a sport, join an intramural sports team, like club softball. This is a great way to stay in shape, expand your social network, and maintain your athletic skills in a particular sport.

**11. Religious:** There is a group for just about *every* religion on most college campuses. This is a great way to stay connected to your religious base and find local houses of worship.

As you can see, there are a zillion things you can get involved with on campus. There are so many things I did not mention, such as: the marching band, becoming a student teacher, teaching assistant, research assistant, or outreach and peer education representative, joining the Reserve Officers' Training Corps (ROTC), becoming involved with groups focused on a hobby, like ballroom dancing—and the list goes on and on. Most schools have a Website or other listing of all the campus organizations. Figure out where you fit. Also keep your eyes open for flyers and postings of things going on around campus.

**Side Note #1:** Besides being involved in organizations, you should **get involved politically,** meaning follow the presidential and local government election, and *vote!*

**Side Note #2: Read the New York Times, Washington Post, or a highly reputable national newspaper at least on Sunday.** Try to read whatever daily, weekly, or monthly trade journal there is in your field. You should also read your campus newspaper. You want to stay current on what is happening on campus as well as in the rest of the world. Campus definitely becomes your world and it is easy to begin living in a bubble, but you have to be able to engage in discussion on current events and breaking news. You can read many of these periodicals online, but some do charge a fee. You can also check out online news sites as well.

**Side Note #3: Schedule time to volunteer at least once a month.** A benefit of many of the organizations I have already mentioned is that there is a service component that comes with membership. Additionally, scholarships are often available for students with lots of community service involvement.

**Side Note #4: Do not over commit yourself.** (Please see section on "Superwoman Syndrome" later on.) I want you to keep your grades at the forefront of whatever you do. Also, it is not the quantity of your involvement but the quality of your involvement. You don't have to do *everything*! If you try, you will burn out. For example, there is no need to join twenty different organizations and just be a member. Find two or three groups and be a valuable member in those organizations.

You should strive to secure a leadership position in at least one of these organizations. Stay committed to the organization and run for an executive position. Have the courage to try, and if at first you don't succeed, you know the rest. So if you do not win the election the first time around, run again for the same position during the next open election, or run for another position in another organization. In college, I saw the same exact people run for Student Government Association president year after year. Some never won, but at least they can say they gave it their best shot. If you lose the election, maybe you didn't necessarily do anything wrong, but perhaps the other person really was more qualified for the position. Therefore, the position wasn't for you and you learned skills that you can apply to your next run for office.

Another option is to reinstate a former organization or start your own. Now, reinstating or starting your own organization is not easy at all. In fact, unless you are truly passionate about the cause and have a number of reliable people on your executive board to support you, I would steer away from that endeavor. It is a *huge* time commitment and if you have a very tedious course load, it can get intense. You know yourself best, so consider the time you are willing and able to commit to this endeavor. Starting or reinstating an organization can be very rewarding. You see an organization grow from the bottom up, but if your grades are suffering as a result, it may not be worth it.

## Avoid Succumbing to the "Superwoman Syndrome:"

During the spring semester of my junior year in college, I thought I was superwoman. I thought I could do everything. I was on two campus organization executive boards as the president of one organization and the vice president of another. I was also an RA, had an internship that equated to a twenty-hour work week plus an additional nine-hour weekly commute. I was taking fifteen credit hours, had a boyfriend, and had just turned twenty-one. Although I was only a junior, I already had senioritis and guess what? I was a walking ball of stress. Life is too short to be so stressed and overcommitted. Enjoy college and remember to strike a balance with everything you do. Stress is never fun, so avoid the Superwoman Syndrome at all costs! Also, remember what I said in the chapter on maintaining a high GPA from the start: Let your main focus be on achieving a high GPA. **Let your involvement in an organization come second to your grades.**

# So what did you learn about getting involved?

- Getting involved early on shapes your leadership, communication, networking, time management, and public speaking skills.
- There are a zillion organizations on campus; find something you like.
- Get involved politically.
- Secure a leadership position within an organization.
- Read the *New York Times*, *Washington Post*, or a highly reputable national newspaper at least on Sunday.
- Schedule time to volunteer at least once a month.
- Do not over commit yourself.
- Avoid succumbing to the "Superwoman Syndrome."
- Keep your grades at the forefront of whatever you do.

# Tip #6: Get Summer Internships

## (to secure a full-time job *before* graduation)

Ladies, **the competition is fierce!** Think about it; there are millions of students graduating from high school. Somewhere around half of that population will be entering college. Then a large percentage of those graduates will be entering the work force. You have to make sure that you are in a leading position among your peers when it is time to find a good job. This means that you have to ensure that you have a winning resume, strong interview skills, and perform well during your internships.

The reality is that **you are not guaranteed a job when you graduate.** Maybe you will get your first job offer during your junior year or maybe you'll graduate and won't find a job until a year later. Many factors are in play. Three of the most important factors are the job market, your preparation, and your commitment to not giving up. Since you cannot control the job market, it would be in your best interest to be as prepared as possible.

Having strong internship experience is one of the key ways to distinguish yourself among your peers. Internships are so important for so many reasons that I could devote an entire book to that topic alone. There are going to be summers that you want to do absolutely nothing but sleep, but this is not a wise move at all. Take full advantage of the summers by obtaining an internship.

If you can't find an internship in your major and choose to work, don't aim to "just get a job." Try to get a job with transferable skills. If you are a pre-med major, try to "just get a job" doing something at a hospital, so that even if it isn't practical hands-on experience related to practicing medicine, you are in the hospital environment and may have opportunities to speak to doctors on an informal basis. Have a plan of action for your summers during college. Again, having an internship is your best bet. This will help you to determine what you actually like and dislike among the various career paths your major can take you. Many students have changed their major after an eye-opening internship experience. It's much better to figure out some of your likes and dislikes as they relate to your career, while you are still in school so that you still have time to explore other career options.

I decided to get into action by securing an internship the summer after my freshman year. It was around that time that I solidified my major. I began to formulate ideas on how to get an internship in the accounting field to ensure that accounting was what I really wanted to do. I decided to major in accounting after taking a summer course in the subject. When I returned to campus and began considering internships, I knew that before beginning my internship search I had to work on improving my resume. The involvement portion of my resume needed some work. I also needed to keep a high GPA and get a leadership position. So I got involved with an organization and ran for a leadership position within the organization after one semester.

**Side Note #1: Start thinking about your professional career early in your college career!** Be on a constant quest to improve your skill set as it relates to your chosen profession. This includes your resume and interview skills. If resume submissions begin in November, there is no reason why you cannot begin submitting your resume in September or October. Internship slots fill up fast. Get on your grind in researching and applying for internships during the fall preceding the summer you would like to intern. You can even begin developing relationships with recruiters much earlier in your college career so that your resume stands a greater chance of being moved to the top of the pile.

**Side Note #2:** Beginning your freshman year, you should be very familiar with the location of the career center and should begin to develop relationships with the people that work in the center so that when new opportunities arise, you will be one of the first people they consider. No one is going to hand-deliver an internship to you (unless you are *that* connected). You will have to work for it!

**Co-ops:** Co-ops allow you to alternate coursework and employment. For example, out of the full academic year, you may work one semester and take classes the following semester. Co-ops are like an extended internship. As opposed to just interning in the summer when the workload might be less, co-ops give you very practical hands-on experience during the fall or spring and give you a great idea of how working full-time will be when you graduate. Co-ops allow you to earn good money if you need to cover the costs of tuition; however, you probably will graduate a semester later than you initially anticipated.

### The Resume

Your resume is *extremely* important! This is what the employers and recruiters initially see and how they make an assessment of you and your fit with their organization. The best starting point for a resume is a resume book or online resources. The question to keep in mind as your resume is evolving is: **Does this piece of paper make me look *outstanding?*** If not, reword your bullet points, and think of some things you may have forgotten. Your resume should highlight certain points that are consistent with the type of job or internship you are attempting to acquire. For example, if you are looking for a management job, your resume should highlight skills that a manager would have, such as leadership skills and supervisory experience.

**The First Step: Create Your First Resume**

**Create your first resume and then go through the rest of this chapter to make the appropriate changes.** Once you research resume examples you will see that some resume formats are better than others, but keep in mind that no one format is the perfect format. It is ultimately up to you.

When I created my first resume, I did what most students do: I used the resume template within Microsoft Word and just filled in the appropriate fields. Name, address, job title, and job description. Simple and easy. The next day I went to a career fair at my school, ready to hand out my resume to secure an internship. I walked up to the first table, which happened to be the table of an organization known as INROADS.

INROADS is an organization that links minority undergraduate students with summer internships in corporate America. The internships are with well-recognized companies and they are usually well paid. INROADS also provides professional development through ongoing training and monitoring throughout the internship experience as well as the academic school year. There are other organizations similar to INROADS that link minority students of various majors with internships. Go to your school's career center to investigate how to apply to these programs.

The INROADS representative looked at my resume and said, "You used the template, didn't you?" As the timid sophomore that I was, I said "Yes." She went line by line telling me what I did wrong. I left the career fair, ran back to my room, and made all the changes she suggested. When I got back to the career fair, she was not there, but I *had* to find her. I found out that she was going to be a part of a panel at the campus cultural center later on that afternoon discussing ways to secure an internship. I was there before the program began and handed my resume to her. Within a few days, I received a phone call, and had a phone interview with an INROADS representative. Once I became a part of the organization, they provided me with professional development, and soon after, there was an overflow of interview and internship offers.

**Lessons learned? 1. Be persistent! 2. Accept constructive criticism 3. Resumes evolve over time.** A resume is not something you work on for the first time the night before the career fair. I was fortunate to meet an INROADS representative who guided me in the right direction. Check with professionals and career counselors at your college or university and ask for their advice and guidance.

The first resume you create won't look *anything* like the resume you graduate with. You are constantly adding more things you are involved with on campus and fluctuations in your GPA, while constantly deleting more and more things that relate to your high school experience. Only during your freshman year and maybe first semester sophomore year should you still be including high school accomplishments, that is unless you were *stellar* in high school and have absolutely nothing to put on your resume regarding your college experience.

Many people will have different opinions on what looks good on your resume and what does not. I would recommend that you always listen, especially if it's an employer, professor, or parent. In time, you will decide what you really want to keep in tact, no matter how many times someone tells you to change it, and what things you are willing to alter.

**Key point for resume effectiveness. The 3 Cs: Clear, Consistent, and Concise.** For resume clarity, make sure that your job intentions are clear. Someone should be able to read your resume and determine that you are looking for an internship at a law firm. Therefore, your objective, education, and bullet points should highlight qualities, skills, and experience that would indicate that you are a perfect candidate for an internship with that particular law firm, and nothing completely opposite.

When questioning what to include and exclude from your resume, include information that is relevant, timely, and adds credibility. For example, if you are concerned that your one page resume will become two pages and you are applying for a position as a manager for a retail store, your stint as a dishwasher of a restaurant in junior high school can be left off of your resume.

For resume consistency, be sure to make your resume easy on the eyes. That means a font and layout that is not too jumbled and sloppy. Use the same font, bullet points, and indentations throughout. Make sure margins and tabs are aligned. If you bold one job title, bold all job titles. If you refer to the time frame you held a job as "summer 2007" don't use "July 15, 2006–August 23, 2007" later on. Be consistent.

The last C is for concise. **Resumes should be one page.** No one has the time or interest to read a multiple page resume at your level. Only someone with an extensive professional career should exceed one page. There may be specific rules for you major and/or industry where you will include a portfolio or a submission package that exceeds one page. Research this information early on.

**Branding:** Be sure to brand your resume. If you interned at a prestigious firm, put their name on it. If you worked on high profile clients, put that on your resume as well. If you interned at a popular not-for-profit organization or participated in a well-known community service activity, mention it.

**Side Note #3:** The purpose of a resume is to get the interview. Your goal then is to grab the reader's attention as quickly as possible, so listing outstanding accomplishments toward the top of your resume works to your advantage (see section on "Order of Wooage" within this tip).

**Resume Format**

**Name (large, centered, and bold)**

**E-mail address**

| | |
|---|---|
| **Current contact info/school info** | **Permanent/home information** |
| **Telephone number (school or cell)** | **Telephone number (home)** |

**Education:** University/College name and degree attained or expected graduation.

The name of the school within your university, such as The William H. Scott School of the Arts. Any special/scholarly/study abroad programs you participated in, such as if you were in an honors program. Your major and minor (if you have a minor). Your major GPA, cumulative GPA, or both (and the scale used, i.e. a 4.0 scale would read 3.8/4.0).

**Honors/Awards/Scholarships,** name of award and date received.

**Jobs/Work Experience:** Internships/jobs, time frame you held the position, title of the position. Use bullet points to highlight what you did during each internship/job. Use action words (verbs) such as developed, supervised, responsible for, obtained, created, facilitated, maintained, assisted, trained, and coordinated to begin each sentence. You should use about three to five bullets per job. Any more than that might be too much. Be consistent with the amount of bullets you use for each job. You shouldn't have eight bullets for one job, and one bullet for another job. You don't have to have the same amount of bullets for every job, but again, keep it in the three to five bullet point range.

**Leadership/Activities:** List the organization, your leadership title, and timeframe you held the position.

**Community Service**

**Computer Skills**

**Language Skills**

## Resume Format in More Detail

**Contact Information:** You want the recruiter or employer to be able to reach you, so be sure to include your permanent and temporary contact information. Your e-mail address should be professional. A good standard professional e-mail address is firstnamelastname@xyz. com. This means no trashy e-mail addresses like hotsweetlips@xyz.com or anything with a weird combination of letters and numbers that is prone to be misspelled. An inappropriate e-mail address lessens your credibility.

**Side Note #4:** Whatever the phone number is that you provide on your resume, keep in mind that recruiters and other company representatives will call you at that number and leave messages for you to return their calls. **You should have a standard message,** such as, "Hello. You have reached Candice Jones. I am not in right now to receive your phone call. Please leave your name, number, and a brief message and I'll get back to you at my earliest convenience." Also, be conscious of background noise when answering phone calls from unfamiliar numbers. You do not want the recruiter hearing the loud party going on in your dorm room when they are calling to set up an interview.

**GPA:** If your cumulative GPA is below a 3.0, you may want to only include your major GPA if it is higher than your cumulative GPA, or not put your GPA on your resume at all.

**Internships/Jobs:** Try to make your job title much more interesting than just "Cashier" or "Intern" but don't make it so fancy that you lose the essence of what you really did. "Lead Cashier" sounds better than "Cashier." "Marketing Intern" sounds better than "Intern".

**Bullet Points:** Be sure to include number values where possible, to quantify the value you added in that role. For example, "assisted 300–400 customers daily," "increased revenue by 40 percent by doing x,y,z," "responsible for thirty-two residents." This allows the person reviewing your resume to make a tangible assessment of the value you added to that organization during that particular time frame.

**Leadership/Activities:** You can choose to have a leadership section, an activities section, or a section that combines both to list your extracurricular activities. As I stated in Tip #5, "Get Involved Early On," strive to run for a leadership position on campus because it builds several skills, like your leadership and public speaking abilities. As I mentioned in Tip #4 "Choose the Right Major for You," be sure to join the campus organization affiliated with your major. The activities section of your resume will include organizations you are a member of but not necessarily one in which you hold a leadership position.

**Side Note #5:** Join a national organization affiliated with your profession, such as the National Association of Social Workers if you are pursuing a degree in social work. If you are looking for a space-filler (meaning your resume has way too much space), you can also list professional conferences you have attended while in college, especially those you were specially selected to attend for your academic achievements.

**Community Service:** Add a few major community service actives you have participated in. Remember what I said about resume branding: People like to identify with things they are familiar with. So let's say you participated in a National AIDS walk; list it! Perhaps your interviewer participated in the exact same AIDS walk.

**Computer Skills:** If you know a computer software system that is unique to your profession, be sure to include this on your resume. If you know computer coding or systems like C++ or Java, then add this as well.

Microsoft Office, which includes Microsoft Word, PowerPoint, Excel, and Access, should be added if you are proficient in these applications, but if you begin running out of space, make this section the first to be removed. Many employers expect students graduating from college to be proficient, if not extremely familiar, with these applications.

**Language Skills:** Knowing a foreign language, such as Spanish or French, is great! One word of caution: Do not lie and say you are fluent, semi-fluent, or conversational in a language if you are not. Do not lie on any part of your resume; realize that lying about a language in particular may come back to haunt you when you are hired. This is especially true if you are hired under the condition that you can assist the organization in translating this language.

**References:** There is no need to have "references upon request" at the bottom of your resume. If you need to provide references, the employer will ask you for them.

**Objective vs. No Objective?** An objective is not mandatory, but if you use one, be specific. Avoid using overly flowery and verbose language. Be direct and to the point. You can have several versions of your resume with different objectives, tailored to the varying types of jobs you are applying for. You should tailor the rest of your resume to be aligned with your objective. For example, if you are a communications major and looking for an advertising internship, your objective should specify that you are looking for an advertising internship, and the bullet points associated with your work experience should highlight the skills that are most relevant for an advertising internship, such as your project management and creativity.

**Tailoring Your Resume:** No matter what your work experience may seem to indicate, *any* experience can be translated into the experience needed for your next job. You must focus on pulling out skills that can be translated into doing the new job successfully. The skills you acquired at your last job or series of jobs are transferable. Work on your word usage and have others review your resume to ensure you are not stretching the truth.

**Order of "Wooage:"** How do you woo someone? By leaving a great impression. When a recruiter reads your resume from top to bottom, you want to grab their attention as early as possible. In other words, you want to woo them as early as you can. Ask yourself what is most impressive on your resume? Is it your honors and awards? Leadership positions? Or did you have an internship at a reputable firm? Whatever stands out as the best is what needs to be highlighted closest to the top of your resume. For a college student, your contact info and education should always be first, but you can change the order of the rest of your resume. Put whatever is strongest first and order the rest of the resume in descending order of wooage. For example, Shelly has no internship experience, but is an RA and won RA of the year. Her resume should have her name and contact info, education, leadership positions (RA), honors and awards (RA of the year), and then experience.

**Final Resume Pointers:**

1. **Put your resume on resume paper.** This paper has a much thicker consistency than regular white paper. Stick to natural tones such as white, off white, and cream.

2. **If you worked to finance some of your education, include this information.** "Worked forty-plus hours weekly to finance one hundred percent of education." If you have to work that many hours in a week and you have maintained a high GPA, you are very impressive.

3. **Should you list your qualifications and skills?** No, I think someone should be able to tell just by reading your resume what your qualifications and skills are. If you held leadership positions, it is clear that you are a leader. If you worked forty-plus hours a week to finance your education, you are a hard worker with a strong work ethic. If you have a high GPA, you have mastered the material and you are probably smart/intelligent. There is no need to have a separate section listing your qualities at a college level. Once an interview is granted, someone will be able to make that

assessment of you. If you are adamant about listing your qualities somewhere, list and discuss those skills in your cover letter.

4. **For current jobs, when wording your bullet points, be sure to use present tense (assist), and for past jobs use past tense (assisted).**

5. **Should you list relevant coursework?** Maybe. Many students list the classes they have taken thus far in their major on their resume. If you are a freshman and need a space filler, then okay, add this section. For sophomores and above, you should be able to find something much more valuable to add to your resume. Most undergraduates in a particular major take similar classes, so that does not make you stand out among your peers. If you have taken a supplemental course that is unique to your school, then definitely add it! I would create a "Specialized Coursework" section. For example, almost all engineering majors have to take particular core engineering courses. Now if you took another course in fire engineering, you can add this course to your resume because it is specialized and unique. This information on your resume can lead to discussion points during an interview.

6. **Avoid red flag words** such as "union." If you are the president of the union at your job, you may want to refrain from putting that information on your resume. Unions are a lifesaver for many professionals; however, the word often has a militant undertone.

7. **Your cover letter should be addressed to a specific person.** Do not address it "To Whom It May Concern." Look online for examples of cover letters. Many jobs I encountered in college did not require cover letters, but some do and it's the same drill. No typos! Be clear on the position you are interested in. This is the opportunity to list your qualities. When listing your qualities, review your resume and be sure that the qualities you highlight on your cover letter are aligned with your resume. You should not say in your cover letter that you are a leader and when the recruiter looks at your resume, you have held no leadership positions. Try to pull adjectives that your resume clearly identifies.

8. **Know your resume inside and out** and have strong examples of experiences that you can draw good examples from during the interview.

9. **Again, don't stop until you sound absolutely outstanding!**

10. Last, but certainly not least: **Proofread your resume a million times,** and have family members, friends, and professors offer their opinions. Realize that everyone's opinion will vary, so listen to the critiques and figure out what you agree with and what you want to leave as it is.

## The Second Step: The Interview

**Preparation Before the Interview:**

**Attire:** Know the attire for your job environment. Aim for a classic and conservative look, despite the job and industry. For example, when interviewing for a super conservative finance internship, aim for a high-quality skirt-suit in a dark color such as navy blue. Have shined (non-dusty) shoes. Don't wear big gaudy earrings or other excessive jewelry, and keep your hair away from your face. Have skin-toned panty hose and avoid extra long finger nails, beads in your hair, or super high (overly sexy) stilettos. For a less conservative PR interview, keep it conservative, but perhaps add a bit of your own flavor to the ensemble. If you are having difficulty determining if your look is appropriate or not, I would ask a parent, professor, or career counselor for an opinion. Have fresh breath, but no gum or candy should ever be in your mouth before or during the interview.

**Research the company online.** Make sure you have researched the company's core values and have determined that their values tie into your own personal values. During the interview, tie their values to your work and academic experience to express how you are a great fit with that particular organization. You can cite specific examples of how you have exemplified these values in your academic experience and extracurricular activities.

**Research the type of interview style generally used in that particular profession.** For example, the majority of my interviews were behavior-based interviews. I knew of students looking for finance internships that were asked specific question related to certain financial terms. If you know the type of interview, you can ensure you are adequately prepared by practicing sample questions. A method I used, once I knew my interview was going to be behavior-based, was to do an Internet search for "behavior based interview questions." I then sat in front of my computer and answered the questions to the computer screen as if I were really in an interview. An example of a behavior-based question is "Tell me about a time when you had to work with difficult team members and how you were able to handle it."

There are many other types of interviews such as stress and brain teasers. Stress interviews are intended to get you frazzled. Your interviewer may choose a random object and say, "Sell this item to me as if I were a prospective customer." Brain teasers are also tough. I have seen students applying for some consulting positions have to undergo these types of interviews. An example of a brain teaser interview question is "How many gas stations are there in the United States?" Your answer does not necessarily have to be correct. They just want you to logically think through an answer and come up with a general number range, but it's your rational thought process that they are trying to assess. Talk to people who have interviewed with the companies with which you will be interviewing. They can tell you the questions that they were asked.

**Prepare at least three questions for the interviewer.** Have good, thought-provoking questions to ask at the end of the interview. You should tailor the questions to who is interviewing you. If it's a human resources representative, ask questions tailored to the training you will receive or specific questions related to the internship that they did not cover in the company presentation. If your interviewer is an employee, ask them specific questions related to their career path and day-to-day job responsibilities.

**Practice interviewing with family, friends, or a counselor.** Be passionate about the position. Act as if you really want the job! Project your voice! Even if you are meek and shy, this is not the time for that. Your vocal projection is of extreme importance in an interview. If organizations on campus are offering free mock interview or "dress for success" sessions, take advantage of these opportunities! This will be a great chance for you to practice and get feedback on your interview performance and attire. The only way to get good at interviewing is by interviewing! The only way to know you are dressed appropriately is to see appropriate dress.

**Side Note #6:** Depending on the size of the organization, you will probably be interviewing with more than one person. They could all be back-to-back or they could be over the course of several weeks. If you make a mistake in one of the interviews, try to avoid that slip-up during any of the remaining interviews. Also, remember to be passionate in all of your interviews.

**Prenight Reception/Dinner:**

Many companies have prenight receptions the day prior to the interview as an opportunity for you to meet other employees at the firm or to meet who you'll be interviewing with the following day. Realize that from the prenight reception, your interview, and internship, this is an ongoing interview process. You are constantly being assessed. Your interaction at the prenight reception can help or hurt you. If available, be sure to attend an etiquette dinner or two sponsored by a campus group to polish your skills, prior to embarking on company-sponsored dinners. At the prenight reception, do not wait for someone to come up to you. Approach others with confidence, introduce yourself, and ask follow-up questions.

## Day of the Interview:

**Arrive on time** (meaning fifteen minutes early; not *too* early though). Have your entire physical package looking good. Come with several copies of your resume, especially if it has been updated. Get a portfolio in which to place your resumes. Remember that your appearance is one of the most important aspects of the interview.

## Right Before the Interview:

Greet the receptionist with respect. Read the company materials provided in the waiting area to learn more about the company. If there are company representatives waiting with you in the reception area, this is also an opportunity for them to assess your fit with the firm. Make sure you talk to these representatives. Regular small talk about the profession is always good. Show your personality in an appropriate but fun manner. Realize that the entire time you are waiting for the interviewer, you are being evaluated.

You may have to fill out a job application right before the interview; therefore, you should bring all the pertinent information, such as past employers' addresses, phone numbers, etc., so you can complete this information onsite. When your interviewer approaches you, stand up and give a firm handshake. Practice your handshake if necessary. Make sure it's not too intense.

**During the Interview:**

The interview is really an opportunity to sell yourself, so be **confident.** Don't just say you are confident; you have to exude confidence. Pretend if you have to. **Make eye contact** without staring. Sit when offered a seat. Avoid excessive fidgeting. Try not to look nervous. Relax your face, wear a tiny smile, and do not nod your head too quickly when agreeing with a statement. You should also never nod your head when answering a question. Sit up straight. Avoid constantly adjusting your attire, crossing your arms across your chest, or placing them on your hip. This gives off a closed demeanor. Cross your legs at the ankles (known as American style). Never cross your legs with one full leg over the other, where your thigh could be exposed (this is known as European style). Laugh beneath the interviewer's laugh when appropriate. No loud outbursts of laughter. Avoid talking negatively about past employers. Slow your words down so that your speech is clear. Students can be extremely nervous during interviews and end up sounding rehearsed and speaking at 1,000 words a minute. Slow down and use simple language. Using complex words makes you sound like you're trying too hard and not very intelligent.

Talk about your accomplishments with pride, but interviewers know when you are boosting a job or position up beyond what it really is. Avoid saying "like" and "um" when you are at a loss for words. You are better off taking a pause and organizing your thoughts about your answer and then proceeding. Use body language to emphasize a point but be careful how much you use your arms to emphasize points because it may block your face or draw attention away from the interview. Remain motivated and show you are really excited about the job. Listen to the question first, and then answer it. Be concise and to the point. Give strong and specific examples. Give an answer and then a story to illustrate trends in your behavior. Don't ask any salary questions; either they will let you know or it will be included in your offer letter. Don't bring up personal facts like the fact that you are a mother of two, a Democrat, and what your views are about war.

**Side Note #7:** Be yourself!

## General Interview Format:

**Two minutes**—establish rapport

**Two minutes**—topic opener

**Twenty minutes**—gather information/accomplishments/ self-appraisal/your direct competency

**Five minutes**—for you to ask questions and for them to respond

**One minute**—summary and close

The questions an interviewer asks you are a direct probe into your skill sets. At the beginning of the interview, the interviewer will introduce herself and throughout the course of the remainder of the interview may make several comments about herself. Pay attention. Formulate two questions based on something that was previously stated, such as, "Could you clarify/explain that point you mentioned earlier about xyz?" Ask the interviewer why they chose the industry/firm. If you were not already told, another question that could be asked is, "What is the next step in the interview process?"

Using your resume as a guide, the interviewer may generally start with general questions like, "So why did you pick XYZ University?" She will generally continue onto specific questions about your internships, jobs, educational experiences, major accomplishments, problems you faced during any of those experiences and how you handled them, as well as your strengths and weaknesses.

**Side Note #8:** Am I being particular? *Yes*! Do you have to follow everything in this chapter verbatim? *No*! I tried to include some additional things that were told to me or acquired from some abstract source that is now in my head, and yes, I followed these things and got a job, so see if it works for you. Now back to the interview...

## After the Interview:

Get a business card, give a firm handshake, and smile. Reiterate your interest in the position. Follow up within twenty-four hours with an e-mail. Make sure you use *spell-check*! And include key phrases like, "I am impressed with the team and role," and "I am confident that I will add value to the team." Many people will tell you to send a hand-written note, which is up to you, but in this day and age of technology, an e-mail is fine. For some positions, by the time a note reaches your interviewer, the position will probably have been filled already.

## The Lunch or Dinner After the Interview:

The following information can also be applied to the prenight reception previously discussed. Try to figure out what you want on the menu quickly. Order what you want, but don't go overboard and order the $55 meal when everyone else's meal is in the $10 range. Order "safe" meals, meaning no spaghetti! Let the host order first, unless they insist you order first. In terms of eating bread at the table, tear off a small piece and butter it pieces at a time. In terms of shared sauces, spoon some onto your plate. Avoid dipping and redipping. Rest your silverware down when speaking; don't leave silverware dangling in the air.

If you need to leave the table and go to the bathroom, there is no need to announce where you're going, just say, "Excuse me," and put your napkin on your seat. Always avoid controversial topics such as politics and religion at the table. **Wait for everyone to get their meals and then wait for your host to begin eating. That's your queue that you can start.** If you need something from across the table, ask politely for someone to pass it to you. No eating with fingers. Therefore, do not order food which requires your hands and no silverware, like ribs or fried chicken.

## How Do I Actually Get the Contacts I Need to Get an Internship?

### 1. Online Databases:

Each university should have a career Website where you are given the opportunity to upload your resume and apply to internships and jobs posted by various employers. These sites have a search engine where you can search for jobs and internships. Hopefully they have search criteria that allow you to specify the internships you are looking for such as by major, geographical region, part-time or full-time. Once you narrow down the search field, apply to as many positions as you are interested in, whether that be five, ten, or thirty. It really just takes a click of a button to hit submit and the employers will usually get back to you in a reasonable time.

**Side Note #9: Don't let rejection stop you.** It happens to the best people at some time or another. The person looking at your resume has no idea how fabulous you are. As a matter of fact, save your rejection e-mails. One day they will want you to work for them and you can say, "Ha, I don't think so!" At that point the choice will be yours.

## 2. Career Fairs:

Career fairs give you a great opportunity to sell yourself. If your GPA is low, now that you have that face-to-face contact, show them the polished professional that you are. Research the companies that will be there and make a plan to visit each one of those tables.

Have several copies of your resume to hand out. Bring the resume that has been tailored to the specific company in which you are interested. Be confident! Extend your hand and give a firm handshake. When you say your name, it isn't "Hi, I'm Sylvia." It's "Hello. My name is Sylvia Jones (soon to be followed by) I am a junior journalism major, particularly interested in learning more about the summer internship opportunities available within your organization," (soon to be followed by a question). The same attire issues I brought up during the interview apply to career fairs as well. Again, have well-groomed hair, a dark professional suit, and no excessive jewelry or makeup. Keep your look classic to be on the safe side. Project your voice and be assertive. Get business cards made for yourself and follow up with the contacts you have made within twenty-four hours via e-mail (check for typos). "I enjoyed meeting you today at The University of XYZ career fair. I am confident my credentials are exactly what you are looking for. I have attached an additional copy of my resume ..."

> **Side Note #10:** If there is a company you know you want to work for and they do not attend your school's career fair, research the career fair schedule of surrounding schools and see if you can attend that particular career fair, or just show up and hope for the best.

## 3. Network:

Think about who you or your parents might know and how you can leverage that relationship. Never underestimate the relationship you have with your neighbor who happens to be a criminal lawyer—the very aspect of law you were considering as a profession. You may have to create an internship from scratch by sharing your career interest with your neighbor and your desire to get hands-on experience, even if it's unpaid. Expand your desire for an internship to family, friends, neighbors, teachers, and your church family as well. When an adult asks you how you're doing, make sure you have an answer prepared to market yourself and let them know what you're looking for internship-wise. Surprisingly, people are always willing to help students, particularly those that seem very ambitious.

**4. Go Out On a Limb:**

You have nothing to lose. Let's say your goal is to work at the most popular radio station in your city. Apply! No posted internships available? Use your contacts! No contacts at the radio station? Visit the radio station's Website and see if you can get the name of the human resources contact. Research the bigwig responsible for interns and new hires. Call and try to set up an informational interview with an on-air personality.

An informational interview is an interview where you interview a person, which means that you are the one that asks questions to a professional to learn more about their career and field. Informational Interview Rule #1: Don't ask for a job right after the interview. This interview might be in person, but it can also be on the phone. You are truly gathering information about the profession. Coming in and then asking for a job makes you look a bit deceptive, like you made an attempt to set up your own personal interview. Make a list of potential prospects that you have identified through references or the Internet and begin calling and requesting informational interviews!

## 5. Volunteer:

Let's say you are a psychology major and would really like to get a taste of what it would be like to run your own private practice. If you cannot find an internship or job that will give you the exposure you are looking for, volunteer your services without compensation.

## The Offers

If you get only one internship or job offer, you should probably take it, but if you get several offers you may be deliberating which one to accept. The answer is you should take the position that will place you in the best situation professionally. Choose the internship that will give you the experience you truly want, or maybe it's a combination of the experience and name recognition you need. The offer letter usually has a deadline. Don't miss that deadline. Be sure to read through the accompanying information they usually send with your offer letter, such as information about the company, special programs, perks, and health benefits.

## The Third Step: You've Got the Internship

For many majors, internships will be unpaid. Vary your applications with paid and unpaid internships. If you are financing your tuition and you *have* to have a source of income over the summer months, perhaps accepting an unpaid internship is out of the question, but keep in mind that some of the best internships will come in the unpaid form. Now if it is unpaid, see if your school will give you course credit for the experience. During college I interned for a government agency, got paid, and received three credits, so see if you can reap dual benefits as well. All I had to do was get a good evaluation and write a paper at the end of the semester.

## During the Internship

During one of my internships, a leader in the organization told me, "Get comfortable being uncomfortable." There is such truth behind that statement. Internships can be valuable learning experiences, but they can also be extremely intimidating and uncomfortable. Most people say they want to grow but when faced with a new and challenging situation in which they will grow, they are scared to death. It's normal to feel this way, but just give it your best shot. Your goal is to leave that internship having them think, "We have to hire her!" Perfect the art of listening and observing others. Be like a sponge, absorbing the behaviors, mannerisms, and unspoken rules of the profession. Always be prepared to answer the question, "So what are you working on?" You never know when someone will pop that question on you. As mentioned before, this is an ongoing interview. Everything that you say or do is being observed by someone. Remember why you are there. Be yourself, remain professional, arrive at work on time every day, stay late if necessary, be cordial and friendly at all times, and do a really good job! Your attitude is the most important element in making a good impression. Be the girl that has a winning personality and produces quality work.

Don't be "that girl" in a negative way. You don't want to be the girl that every authority figure can't stand. On the flip side, I don't want you to be the constant people-pleaser either. But if being yourself means having a bad attitude whenever someone asks you to go and make a photocopy or run an errand, then yes, become someone else. Be the girl that photocopies with a smile on her face. As mundane as certain tasks in your internship may be, get over it—they need to be done. Your attitude and the quality of your work are most important during an internship.

**Attire:** Everything I mentioned in the "Interview" and "Career Fair" sections on attire apply here as well. Be well groomed and dressed for your environment. If your work environment is jeans and a T-shirt everyday, still be classy and err on the conservative side. If other employees wear their jeans with holes in them, don't wear your jeans with the holes in them as well. You do not want to stand out in the wrong way. Don't let your outward appearance do the talking for you.

Never use the company phone for long personal calls. Calling home once a day is not the end of the world, but calling all your family long distance to another country is a problem. Don't surf the net, or keep such activity to a minimum. Even if it's just to check your external e-mail account several times during the day, it may just be your luck that as soon as you decide to check your account, your supervisor walks by and notices you're not doing anything work related. If you are a hard worker and have proven yourself, it's not a big deal at all. If you are already on shaky ground, this can only make their impression of you worse.

If there is no work to be done, create work! This is after you have asked *everyone* you can possibly think of if they have work you can help them with. Just ask, "I have free time. Do you need help with anything?" If you see a process that can be much more efficient, come up with a solution. For example, let's say you can add your technological savvy to short-cut a process; propose it to your boss and get some feedback. Under no circumstances should you waste away each day surfing the net or chatting online.

Although you may feel more comfortable with people of a similar ethnicity, don't limit your network. Try to interact with people of all races, cultures, and levels. Don't be afraid to be the only black person in a group. Likewise, do not feel as if you cannot interact with those of the same race as you. Bear in mind that even when you are in the cafeteria, you never know who is watching and making incorrect assumptions based on the groups' behavior. Develop the ability to get along with different personalities. Have a positive demeanor. Be friendly and enthusiastic. Say good morning. Eat lunch with your team. Genuinely (and respectfully) inquire about people's lives on a surface level. If you see pictures of someone's child in a basketball uniform, inquire what position he or she plays. Perhaps you played the exact same position in high school and you can go on to have a full conversation about that topic with that person.

Stay out of gossip and office politics. Don't take things personally. If someone has a bad day or week and attempts to take it out on you, ignore their behavior and remember why you are there. When people act maliciously towards you, it is something going on inside them and it has nothing to do with you. Respect others time. If you say you'll meet someone at 1:30 p.m., be there at 1:25 pm or at least call if you cannot make the appointment. Network. Remember that all relationships are important.

**Balance out being assertive and coming across as if you think you know everything.** The great news is that colleges and universities are providing you with tons of knowledge. The down side is that college students think they know *everything*, so tend to talk lots and listen little. You know some stuff and should express your knowledge by asking probing, well thought-out questions, but never act as if you are smarter than everyone. Offer your opinions and suggestions without appearing arrogant.

**Side Note #11:** This will also ring true when you come home on break. **After taking one class in psychology, do not ordain yourself as the family psychologist.**

Know when to shut up. Mistakes will happen, so give yourself permission to learn and grow. Don't be too tough on yourself and dwell on them. You are a newbie and are unaware of the power and bureaucracy in the organization. Observe and soak it all up. You may make a huge error that is hopefully fixable. You may make a small mistake like saying the wrong thing at the wrong time. The worst thing you can do is to replay these past mistakes in your head. You are young and human; they've probably seen worse. Learn from your mistakes and continue to push forward.

**Get Mentors:** (see Tip # 9: Get Mentors), whether they are formal or informal. Your company may have a mentorship system in place. If it does not and you like someone's professionalism and style, you can introduce yourself and make an effort to get to know them. Mentors are critical to your success.

When you need direction on a task, ask thought provoking questions. Compile a list of a few questions first and then go to your supervisor with several questions at once instead of interrupting them with a question every five minutes. With this tactic, you will probably eventually figure out the answers to some of your questions on your own.

Keep a record of what you have done at your internship. This serves as a great resource when it is time to update your resume. Additionally, if a supervisor needs a refresher of what you actually worked on over the course of your internship, this serves as evidence of what you worked on. If you don't agree with a certain performance appraisal, this can be substantial evidence of your contributions to the organization. Give your all, whether the internship is paid or unpaid!

I just mentioned feedback, which is an important topic. No one likes criticism and no one likes a poor performance appraisal. Always do the best you can and ask for feedback throughout the internship so that you know what you can do to improve. If you believe that your performance is much better than your supervisor believes, try not to get upset. Talk to your supervisor about your appraisal and the areas you strongly disagree with, but do a personal assessment: Did you show up to work late everyday, talk on the phone and surf the net, or did you come in early, stay late, turn in projects on time, ask questions, and do a great job? If your boss is totally wrong, when you do have your conversation, come with supporting evidence to be able to explain the reasons you disagree with their assessment of you.

**Side Note #12:** Get a letter of recommendation from your supervisor before you leave the internship. You don't know if he or she will be there by the time you really need it.

**Side Note #13:** Last but not least, get on your grind when it comes to your grades, getting your resume together, and going on as many interviews as possible. Do not wait until the end of your senior year to try to get an internship. The goal is to secure internships that expose you to your career field and potentially lead to a full-time offer before graduation.

## Are you ready for your homework assignment?

Reread this chapter on summer internships *multiple times*! There is so much information in this one chapter that a "So what did you learn?" feature would be a shortcut to information that is invaluable to your career success. I want you to get out there and take over the world in your particular profession, so do yourself a favor and *reread* this chapter!

# TIP #7: STUDY ABROAD

Studying abroad was one of the best decisions I made during my college years. I spent the winter term of my senior year in South Africa and Lesotho (another country in Africa that is landlocked within South Africa). **There is no type of text book learning that can come close to the learning you acquire through travel and hands-on experience.** The world is huge. There is so much more outside your country's borders. **Your school may have a year, semester, summer term, winter term, or even a week abroad. Take advantage of *at least* one of these opportunities.**

I chose South Africa because I was inspired by Nelson Mandela's plight for freedom. After listening to his lecture at my university three years prior, the love he had for his country was contagious. **If you study abroad, choose a country that has a history, culture, and people that interest you.**

The entire time in Lesotho and South Africa I was thinking, "Why in the world didn't I study abroad every year?" No matter what your major is, you can find a course that is applicable to either your major or your general interest. The course in South Africa was called "Exploring World Issues: South Africa and Lesotho." We spent the majority of our twenty-two-day program in Lesotho. There are no words to describe the beautiful landscape and warmness of the people. And I earned three credits for a life-changing experience!

While abroad, we examined the post-apartheid access to many of South Africa's major resources and its effects on Lesotho, including the economy, education, politics, health, and culture. We visited the University of Lesotho for a day. We stayed with host families that treated us as if we were members of their own family. We volunteered at a home for disabled youth. We painted the most magnificent mural to brighten the lives of the disadvantaged children that were all wheelchair-bound. We saw the king's home, rode on ponies, fed chickens, played soccer with local children, danced with a nun, stayed in huts in the mountains, swam in a natural river, saw dinosaur footprints, and climbed to the top of mountains. My favorite moment in the day was coming home and having a conversation with my host mother about various world issues and gaining a new perspective on things. We sure can live in a bubble!

There is a chance you may get a little homesick, but you'll be back in your home country in no time. Learn to be friends with your trip mates. That can make the trip so much more fun. Also, **if you are studying a foreign language, this is a great opportunity to get real practical experience putting that language to use.** You will meet new and interesting people, explore a whole new city and way of life, and most importantly, you will grow! You will see this country through your own distinct lens while contributing your personal, academic, and cultural diversity to this amazing experience. This may be the only time in your life that you can immerse yourself fully in a foreign lifestyle while participating in fun activities for such an extended period of time.

Many students are concerned about the cost of studying abroad, **but sometimes it's less expensive than a semester at your current college or university.** Financial aid can usually be transferred to the program and many scholarships are also available. I paid for study abroad using two external scholarships I received. This covered the tuition, plane ticket, housing accommodations, some meals, excursions, and transportation.

Safety can also be a concern for some students, but **you are with other students and experienced faculty and staff who are there to lead and supervise the group.** The only time you may be in danger is if you are going out alone at night. This is a bad move. This is a whole new culture and things that are acceptable in one country may be unacceptable in others. In terms of your physical health, I received shots before my departure and was cautious of certain foods I ate while there. I always drank bottled or boiled water and ate cooked food.

**Side Note #1: Once your interest in studying abroad is peaked be sure to visit your study abroad office so that you know the appropriate deadlines for applications and scholarships.**

I don't know who said it first, but one of my favorite quotes is, "Life is not about the breaths that we take, but the moments that take our breath away." This will definitely be an eye-opening experience. Who knew the world was so big?

# So what did you learn about studying abroad?

- There is no type of textbook learning that can come close to the learning you acquire through travel and hands-on experience.
- Your school may have a year, semester, summer term, winter term, or even a week abroad. Take advantage of at least one of these opportunities.
- If you study abroad, choose a country that has a history, culture, and people that interest you.
- You may get a little homesick, but you'll be back in your home country in no time.
- If you are studying a foreign language, this is a great opportunity to get real practical experience.
- Studying abroad does not necessarily cost a great deal of money.
- Studying abroad is safe.
- Once your interest in studying abroad is peaked, be sure to visit your study abroad office so that you know the appropriate deadlines for applications and scholarships.

# Tip #8: Relationships - Don't Hook Up Too Soon

**Boyfriends:**

If you are surrounded by single aunts, older sisters, or your mom's friends, I'm sure you've heard the phrase, "Honey, a good man is hard to find." So that's why a large number of girls plan on finding a future mate in college. I would advise you not to come in with that expectation or you might pounce on the first thing that shows strong interest (which, by the way, might end up being a huge regret).

You'll probably go through no boyfriends, a handful of boyfriends, or maybe you'll meet one main guy freshman year and you'll stay with him until you graduate. You can also end up getting into one of those sticky "friends with benefits" situations. I would steer very far away from that option. **Remember: Opt to be the girlfriend and never the girl on the side.** This means clarifying your status and avoiding that in between "we act like we're boyfriend and girlfriend but we're really not" situation.

Many girls I know went through a few studs, even more duds, and landed on the prize during their junior or senior year. **What is the prize? Someone who is fun to be around, has common interests, and who respects and appreciates you.** Many of my friends never found the prize by their senior year, or found out their supposed prize was really a booby trap in disguise.

> **Side Note #1:** If you do find the prize, try not to make the relationship consume all of your time to the point that you miss out on fun with your female friends.

> **Side Note #2:** Ladies, just like you wouldn't rule out an upperclassman, don't rule out a guy younger than you, especially if he is mature for his age.

College dating can be frustrating and no matter how many times you wear your femininity on your sleeve, a male interest is nice to have. The two to one ratio of girls to guys on most college campuses doesn't really help the situation out either. I too was conditioned to believe that I would meet my husband in college because where else would I meet him after college? In the club? And since I probably wouldn't have time to get to know a guy like I would in college, would he just be interested in one thing anyway? The truth is that you will meet tons of guys in college. All guys are not the same. Some will be nice, thoughtful, ambitious, and trustworthy. Others will be liars, manipulators, verbal or physical abusers, and will only be interested in that one thing...S-E-X. You will cry, perhaps try to starve yourself, or even threaten to do something even more drastic. You will not be the first to try such measures.

Ride the relationship wave like you always have and if this is your first time in a "real" relationship (i.e. mom and dad no longer escort you to the movies and sit a row behind you), then the relationship wave will be very intense, but do ride on. If he does not turn out to be Mr. Right, I'm sure you will learn some valuable lessons after the experience when you are no longer blinded by what you thought was love. **This too shall pass,** as my mother always says, but in your mind it *is* the end of the world! I'm here to declare that it's not. **Just because you don't meet your husband in college does not mean you're destined for a life of loneliness.** You will meet the man of your dreams one day, but who has time to worry about all that right now anyway?

Yes, college can be isolating at times, especially for those who have a hard time finding their particular niche. After a while, you may seem to be willing to accept just about any guy that breathes just to have someone fill that emptiness that springs up on the weekends when you are so bored you're not quite sure what to do with yourself.

**Side Note #3:** Beware of hookup decisions made out of boredom. In the spring, there is an increased feeling of restlessness known as "spring fever." This is when the weather gets warm, spring is in the air, and students begin to act impulsively. Skirts get shorter, and hanging out and partying become more frequent. This is a prime time for random hookups and reduced studying. This is usually near the end of the spring semester and very close to finals. Don't screw up now!

**A word of serious advice:** Yes, I'm getting really serious right now. As much as you can control it, take the energy that you are devoting to focusing on that particular guy and the new girl he's walking with on campus and focus on the bigger picture: getting the best education possible, maintaining a high GPA, all while being involved and having fun.

Women often allow bad relationships to drain them. They captivate every thought, no matter if you're in class, trying to study, or doing your homework. Your grades can drop, you can get physically ill, and even worse, begin the gradual process of eating away at your self-esteem. The worst part is that he's probably moved on and is maintaining his grades, so why shouldn't you? You cannot afford to let that loser preoccupy your study time, causing you to end up with a C in a class when you really deserved a B. It's not worth it! You are fabulous, smart, and have big goals and dreams to pursue. You have no time for someone who doesn't truly value your worth.

**Side Note #4:** Do you still have that high school boyfriend? See how long it can work, but do not carry over anything from high school unless you are serious.

**Side Note #5:** Certain holidays, especially Valentine's Day, can be lonely for a single girl, especially when in college. It will suck, but the next day will be February 15th, and by that time you'll be well over it. Go out with a couple of your single friends and enjoy the perks of not being committed.

**Side Note #6:** Know that once you arrive on campus, you are considered freshman bait. There are men who prey on "freshman meat." They might be upperclassmen or just men from around the neighborhood. Be very cautious of these animals. Their intent is to take advantage of your freshman naiveté. They are skilled in the art of persuasion and can woo you with their money and fancy cars. Stay away!

It's fine to check out the potential candidates, but when you are new to campus, you are a hot commodity. Once you are a little seasoned and the new freshman class comes along the following year, you will be old meat. To maintain your exclusive status, honor yourself and your values by not messing around with the entire campus! Guys talk to each other just like girls do! Additionally, devoting too much time to a relationship, particularly early on in college, can pull you away from your studies, and that is never a good thing.

## Do Give the Smart and Nice Guys a Chance and Make Sure You are Taken on *Dates* (plural)

Believe it or not, smart and ambitious can be attractive, fun, and a complete sweetheart, but usually, it's not until you are hurt by a jerk that you appreciate these diamonds in the rough. I often talk to my friends about relationships and finding a good guy and under close scrutiny we realize that the good guys are often the ones that are overlooked or considered "too nice." Most of you might be attracted to the bad guy who wears all the designer brands and has all the girls running to his beck and call. Ladies, run away from this guy. (Now, there are rare exceptions to this rule, but do read on.)

It is unfair to generalize, but I have noticed a trend with many of these guys. They are usually so into themselves and have so many women flocking after them that they don't usually treat women as the queens that they are. Why? They don't have to. Now, keep in mind, I am a traditionalist; whether on a college budget or not, a woman must be courted. In more modern terms, women must be dated. Ladies, please avoid the first date booby trap called "let's watch a movie at my place." Many will try this route as they attack the new freshman meat, but you have to be much smarter than that. Let him take you out on the first date. You can probably alternate payments or you can each pay for yourself. That's called "going Dutch." And since times are rough on the wallet during college, this makes sense. Just don't make yourself so easy and overly accommodating. Let a guy put in a little work. You are worth it. In the end, you want someone who will value you, is dependable, has a keen sense of humor, has high goals and ambitions, and encourages you to be a better person. **Always keep your standards high!** Choose a guy who won't limit you and will encourage you to be the best you can be.

**Side Note #7:** Never let a guy call you names and/or disrespect you. This includes physical and verbal abuse. If a guy is constantly picking out your flaws and trying to convince you that you are something that you are not, drop him! Someone who loves you surely wouldn't talk to you in that manner. Also, red flags should go up if a guy is constantly placing a guilt trip on you or fails to ever come through on his promises.

So let's make a strong differentiation: Dating around and sleeping around are two completely different concepts. Dating allows you to identify things you really like and dislike, and the great part is that each guy you date won't be your future husband (Whew! Thank goodness). The college campus has a plethora of highly ambitious and smart guys with good home training, but they may not always be wrapped up in the perfect guy package you imagined them to be in. The last time you checked, were you perfect in *every* way? Girls, please focus on the important qualities. You are looking for a human being, right? Hey you never know, you can meet someone in a class, a study group, on your floor, at orientation, or through a hookup of mutual friends. It is hard not to stress out about this area of your life, especially when your friends have boyfriends, but don't be too hasty; it may block you from meeting the person you were meant to meet. Be yourself. Laugh and pursue your interests. In time he'll come if he's supposed to. If you currently have a good guy, treat him well. Enjoy his company. Have fun and study together. Advise and be there for each other. Treasure this wonderful relationship!

**Side Note #8:** Be cautious of friends that love to give relationship advice. They might tell you to stay with a jerk or to leave a perfectly good guy. Friends can mess you up and steer you in the wrong direction sometimes. Misery loves company, so trust your intuition.

You will be blinded by lust at times. You are human. Learn the lesson you were intended to learn from your experience so that you do not have to experience it again.

Everyone has slip-ups. Get up, dust yourself off, and remember to remain focused on why you are in college, and that is for the education. As a friend once told me, "No boys, just books." That is difficult, but you do have to keep things in prospective. You are young and there are plenty of fish in that big ol' campus sea.

**Side Note #9:** Just because a guy cannot pay for the first date does not mean he is a total loser. Students in college are *broke*. Give him a second chance. This rule also applies if he doesn't have the nicest car in the world. Remember to focus on the inherent qualities of the person.

**Side Note #10:** If you end up choosing not to be taken on dates and instead go and watch the movie in either one of your rooms, be mindful of the message you are sending. Nothing is wrong with you going over to talk or him coming over to talk. Those are some of the best college moments. Go and watch the movie at his or your place if you want to, but know yourself and your hormones. You just don't want to move so fast and fail to savor the "getting to know you" moment. If you take the rushed route, it is likely the relationship will end as fast as it began.

### Get to Know the Guy Before You Progress On To Do Other Things: Don't Hook Up Too Soon

For your parents' sake, I wish I could report that everyone abstains from everything in college—sex, drugs, and lies—but that is not always the case. Do get to know a guy. Become his friend before you progress to anything else. That is why dating is so important and college is a great place to date. See him in his different elements: in class, as a leader on campus, as a mentor to other students, at a party, and in the gym. These are ideal situations, but I know it does not always work out that way. Each relationship is formed and progresses differently, but the initial butterflies do subside and there has to be something there that is stronger for it to last. I wish there was a clear-cut formula, but there isn't one. If you get one point and one point only from this chapter, get this: Try not to move too quickly! Believe it or not, guys like the chase and a *slight* challenge of getting a girl's attention. Most guys refuse to admit it, but I'm convinced. Also, have a life outside of him. If things do move too quickly and the relationship ends up fizzling out, again, learn the lesson(s) you were intended to learn and pick yourself up by the bootstraps. Hopefully you will learn that you can't just let every Tom, Dick, and Harry into your personal life. **Remember how valuable you are.**

There is a tender moment of hurt and vulnerability right after a breakup, which I like to call "Me Time." Embrace it. Treat yourself to a manicure and pamper yourself in other ways. Learn what you really want in a relationship the next time around. In the future, look for a guy who is honest, dependable, determined, kind, and patient. Make sure he values you. Hey, and it's okay to have your moments when you ask yourself, "What in the world was I thinking when I got with him?" It will just add to the knowledge you gain that will transform you into a smart and fearless diva.

**Side Note #11:** Some girls are comfortable approaching a guy and asking him out. If you feel comfortable taking this approach, try it. You may want to invite him to an event on campus or something a little less date-like in the beginning. You can work your way up to this by becoming his friend first and seeing where that takes you. Again, I am a traditionalist so find it difficult to outright ask, "So how about a movie Friday night?" However, we are a new generation and women have definitely become more aggressive, so see what works with your personality.

## Don't Become a Groupie (especially an athletic groupie)

First let me define "groupie." A groupie is a girl or a group of girls that hang around particular guys because of their respective status. That could be football, basketball, nice clothing, Greek fraternity, money, etc. They hang around these guys all the time. They are not the girlfriends but girls that these guys use for sex. They are giddy most of the time, try to reveal too much in their dress, and are constantly aiming to draw attention to themselves so that they will be noticed. There are several motivating factors behind being a groupie. Many girls believe that being around a guy with status increases their status as well. For example, in the case of an athletic groupie, if the athlete goes pro, groupies think they will become the trophy wife.

> **Side Note #12:** Ladies, remember, less is more. There is no need to prance around campus with a full face of makeup and skin-tight jeans that could possibly cut off your blood circulation. If he's going to like you, he should like you without all the adornment.

Now I am not saying *all* of these types of guys are bad. A jerk is a jerk, no matter what. I focus on not becoming an athletic groupie because depending on the school you attend, athletes can really be placed on a pedestal. But again, even on a pedestal, not all athletes are bad. (Feel free to substitute athletes for another type of guy that attracts groupies.) A few of my college friends have had relationships with athletes that continue to this day, but the reality is that athletes often have tons of girls throwing themselves at them who are willing to do whatever, whenever. If you choose to date an athlete, just let the relationship develop as naturally as you would with any regular campus guy. If both of you like each other genuinely, meaning you would be with him even without the athlete status, then things stand a far greater chance of working out. If you are planning to snag a campus athlete for the potential rich and famous lifestyle, keep a couple of things in mind: The majority of the guys you are chasing 1) probably won't become a professional athlete; 2) seem to be the big man on campus now, but outside of the realm of college, they are an average Joe; 3) won't make you his main squeeze or be faithful once he has hundreds of women throwing themselves at him. Hopefully you or your athlete boyfriend aren't taking offensc to all this. Again, a jerk is a jerk, athlete or not. All athletes are not bad, but I am being so real with you right now. I've seen many tears shed and embarrassment caused by an athletic slip-up.

Being the girlfriend of an athlete and being a groupie are two different things. Refer to the first line of this section for the definition of a groupie and do not—I repeat, do not—be a groupie! Once that label is placed on you, it is irreversible. You will always be considered a groupie. Plus you should never have to chase a guy, as groupies often have to do. Set standards for yourself. Outside of your college campus, would you be proud to have him walk by your side? If you were popular in high school and you think this is a means to establish that same popularity in college, choose another option. You have so much to focus on besides trying to get the attention of a guy who is not that interested in you as a person.

## Don't Believe That You Too Can Be the Raunchy Sex-Addicted Character From a TV Sitcom

Many girls fantasize about being the raunchy sex-addicted character from a TV sitcom. In my day, *Sex and the City* was the show to watch. Every female could identify with one of the four leading characters. The sex-addicted character on that show was Samantha. Her lifestyle seemed glamorous and spontaneous. The key word here is "seemed." Although Samantha was fictional, there are many women that lead that type of uninhibited, carefree lifestyle.

Samantha meets a guy in the club and then three hours later Samantha is in bed with him. What a spontaneous lifestyle! What they are not showing is what is happening inside of Samantha. When you continuously give your body frivolously to men, it will eventually eat away at your self-esteem. No matter how much you claim it does not affect you, it does. You will learn a lesson in the process, but I'm a strong believer that you do not have to learn every life lesson through experience. You can learn from the experiences of your friends and family members. Remember to respect your body and yourself. Whether or not you are going to live like Samantha, please protect yourself—and if you do not know what your options are, hop on over to the university health center or a nearby Planned Parenthood and they will let you know all of your options.

Guys are usually very easy to read. If a guy is too busy and doesn't come through the way he promised or you anticipated, you make excuses for him. The entire time, his intentions are very clear. Usually everyone else can see it except you. Yes, college students have abnormal schedules, but if a guy is only calling you after midnight on the weekends, he probably just wants to sleep with you. Do you see how simple it was to come to that conclusion when it's not *you* currently in the situation? Read the signs, ladies. Do not be naïve and make excuses for his behavior.

**Side Note #13:** For all those girls who really just like to have a good time, this is not a public announcement for everyone to live a life of celibacy, especially if that is really not your thing (although it might be the wisest option). I believe all the fun you are seeking will eventually subside and one day you will crave a person you can truly depend on, and who respects and appreciates you. If you know fully what you are getting yourself into and are okay with this arrangement, no one should pass judgment on you. This message is for girls who do not know what they are getting themselves into. If you go through a period of promiscuity, you can always change your behavior. You have that option. You are worth so much more than you think you are. One of my favorite quotes by Maya Angelou says, **"I can be changed by what happens to me, but I refuse to be reduced by it."** You are still a precious gem. Remember to always carry yourself like a classy lady.

## But What If the Guy that Treats Me Like Crap Is the Only One To Make Me Get Out Of My Slump? If Only He'd Act the Way He Used To Act!

No matter how many "girl you need to leave him's" you get, often times the only person you believe can truly console you when you are feeling down about a relationship is the one that said or did the hurtful things to put you in your state of helplessness and self-pity. You say to yourself, "But he was *so* nice in the beginning. I'm not really sure what happened." You hope for him to call and apologize and explain how sorry he is, that he'll never do it again, and how much he loves you. Are you still waiting for that phone call? Or has he called with all of his apologies but hasn't changed his behavior one bit? This is a tough situation and is very subjective. You might have spent an enormous amount of time and energy in the relationship and hate to see it go. But one thing I do know is this: If his words and/or actions become hurtful and disrespectful, you do not need that messing with your head. I don't care if he's going through his own set of personal issues; there is no need to be *rude*.

Unfortunately (or fortunately) the "nice guy" you met in the beginning was a façade and now his true colors are coming to light. The personality he wooed you with might have been a part of a game he plays to pull girls in. You are too mature for games. Behind every tough situation there is a blessing. We are all human and should be given a second or third chance (he's on *very* thin ice at this point), but when is enough enough? Only you can truly call the shots on this one. Remember your focus, your dreams, and your goals. Is he leading you closer to them or farther away?

There are so many negative repercussions of staying in a bad relationship. I hope I have made it clear to you that a bad relationship simply is not worth it. You cannot prevent heartbreak; it just happens. Surround yourself with good friends and throw yourself into activities that really deserve your time and attention. **Connect with your God.** Pray and ask for the strength to get you through this (temporary) storm.

**Side Note # 14:** Don't believe the daily horoscope that reads "prince charming will be in the dining hall today." Must I even explain this one?

**What Happens When I Get Dumped, Especially When He Just Stops Calling and I'm Left Hanging Without an Explanation?**

Most serious relationships (and these include the unofficial ones in which you don't have the official "girlfriend" title as well) will hurt when they do not work out. Take your time to be alone, to cry, and to be sad. It hurts badly, but guess what? You will be okay. You are beautiful and fabulous. What a mistake he made! And who the heck is he to try to make you feel like crap?

It is disrespectful, inconsiderate, and cowardly to just disappear from a relationship. Get a good friend's shoulder to cry on. Only time will heal your wounds. One day you will realize that this was a blessing in disguise. And remember, just because you've been hurt by one, two, or ten men, doesn't mean all men are bad. You'll find a good one when the time is right. Take this time to fall in love with yourself again.

Ladies, relationships can be very time consuming and stressful. If you find a particular relationship is pushing you away from your studies, your goals, or your true self, it's time to reanalyze the situation and determine if this is the type of relationship you want to continue to be in.

**Friendships:**

You've probably been told that the friendships you make in college are usually lifelong friendships and that is very true. These are usually the people you invite to your wedding. Many people bond with those they live with freshman year. You will probably never have this amount of time again in your life to really get to know a person.

Do not despair if you don't form a tight clique early on or if you find just one or two friends. Perhaps your most treasured friendships will be the ones you formed in high school or after college at your first job. Friendships happen naturally and you'll form plenty of them over the next four years. I formed some of my best relationships in campus organizations and summer internships. It's not the quantity of friendships, it's the quality. A really good friend is so hard to find, so if you find one or a couple, consider yourself blessed.

Remember back in the "First Days" chapter when I told you to attend all the freshmen "getting to know you" sessions? Well by now you probably know why. The people you meet earliest on are usually your closest friends. When you start college, many times you hang around girls that are from your former high school or from the same region of the country. Even though you have that commonality, stretch yourself and form friendships with people that are from other regions of the country and the world as well. **In college, you may have to force yourself to develop relationships outside of what seems natural or easy.** That includes friends of a different race, religion, or nationality. You would be surprised to know how much more you are alike with others than you are different. You might even get a bad first impression of a person, but you may be surprised that you actually like the person once you allow yourself to get to know them a bit more.

No matter what, **always surround yourself with go-getters, people who are positive, ambitious, and will be honest and genuinely happy for you.** Birds of a feather really do flock together. Friends can lift you up and friends can pull you down. **Evaluate your friendships and decide who the members are of what I like to call your "dream team."** These are the friends who will be by your side during the good and the bad times and are really interested in seeing you succeed. Your peers have an enormous influence on your behavior and you emulate those with whom you associate most closely. Friends who are focused on having good grades and studying can easily influence you to do the same. If your friends seem to be heading in the opposite direction, don't be afraid to expand your social circle. Don't let friends limit you. If they are remaining stagnant and you are trying to take over the world, you may need to move on. Try not to burn bridges, but remember that not all friendships are forever.

Distance yourself in an appropriate manner because you'll never know when your inappropriate separation will bite you in the butt. Karma is a bummer, but if a relationship isn't working for you—like you often question if a friend is real or true—talk to your friend about it and then trust your gut. This may apply to some of your high school friends whom you have outgrown. You may have dreams and goals that are different from your friends, which is okay. This might just require you to branch out on your own.

One thing I had to learn was that other people are not perfect, and I'm not so perfect either. Therefore, no friendship is going to be perfect. You may be forced to learn the art of forgiveness—forgiving others and asking for forgiveness. Life is too short to hold grudges, but if a relationship is toxic, let it go but forgive them. You don't want to walk around carrying anger and animosity toward anyone. As I mentioned earlier, if someone has done you wrong and has not apologized, she has probably moved on while you are still harboring all this negativity. Don't give anyone that much power over your life! College friendships are about cycles. You will gain plenty of friends and lose a few too. Don't be discouraged by the separation. Some people are intended to be in your life for just a short moment. Learn from the situation. Last but not least, refer back to the tip on having fun. College is so much more fun if you have great friends to share great moments with, so **have fun!**

## So what did you learn about relationships?

- Be the girlfriend and never the girl on the side.
- When choosing a guy, opt for "the prize." That is someone who is fun to be around, has things in common with you, respects and appreciates you.
- No matter the situation, "this too shall pass."
- Always keep your standards high!
- Remember how valuable you are.
- "I can be changed by what happens to me, but I refuse to be reduced by it."
- Connect with your God.
- In college, you may have to force yourself to develop relationships outside of what seems natural.
- Always surround yourself with go-getters, people who are positive, ambitious, and will be honest and genuinely happy for you.
- Evaluate your friendships and decide who the members are of what I like to call your "dream team."
- *Have fun!*

# #9: Get Mentors (THEN BECOME A MENTOR)

**No one in this world has become successful on his or her own.** Every successful person has received guidance from family members, friends, colleagues, or mentors. While in college, I was a part of the National Association of Black Accountants (NABA). One thing I valued tremendously was their adage "Lifting as we climb." They were focused as an organization in breaking professional barriers. Their goal was to move to higher ranks and capabilities in the accounting profession, while simultaneously lifting younger generations to new heights.

You will need a couple of good mentors throughout your college career. Some mentors that are mandatory include:

**1) An upperclassman mentor (preferably in your major)**

**2) The dean, assistant dean, a professor, or other faculty member (preferably in your major)**

**3) Someone you admire and genuinely like (they may not even formally know that you have identified them as your mentor)**

I strongly believe that the more quality mentor relationships you have, the merrier your life will be. Mentors are good at what they do. It's best that you sit there like a sponge and take in all of their invaluable advice so that you can model yourself after them. Also, you won't have to make the same mistakes they made along the way. Mentors have been around the block a time or two and you can learn so much by just listening to how they have handled particular situations. They were in your shoes at some point in their life.

**One thing to keep in mind is that relationships are two-way streets.** You have to cultivate the mentor/mentee relationship by doing your part to keep in touch with your mentor. Hopefully they are going to keep in touch with you as well. Don't make it so that your mentor is doing all the e-mailing and scheduling of dinners and lunches and you're not putting in any of the work to maintain the relationship. Schedule occasional meetings with your mentors to catch up on things. Spend time with your mentors in various environments. Go out to lunch, shop, or catch a movie together. You may feel you have little to give your mentor, but most people enjoy helping others in which they see something special or who remind them of themselves at a point in their life. Make sure you are genuinely concerned with what is going on in your mentor's world as your mentor will probably be concerned with what's going on in yours. Have a goal by the end of your freshman year to know at least one or two faculty members well enough so that they know you and are fully aware of your goals.

**If your mentor offers you constructive feedback, don't go into a defensive mode and block out what is usually really good advice, even if it feels like they are picking on you.** Suck up that sensitivity and make a change in your behavior. Many people will not be honest with you, so if you find a mentor that gives you feedback, cherish this relationship. If you get super defensive, they might not offer you any feedback in the future. Your mentor has the ability to see how one of your negative traits may impede you in the future. Clear it up now or deal with it later. Mentors tend to slap you in the face with a dose of reality by showing you things from another perspective. You have no idea how far that connection will take you.

Mentors can also be your peers. You may like the way one of your peers runs their organization, or perhaps it's the way they handle stressful situations. **Whenever you see someone doing something positive, you can model yourself after them, even if it is just one or two qualities.** If you feel weird asking your peer to be your mentor then this can be an informal mentoring relationship and that person does not even have to fully be aware that you have identified them as your mentor.

One of the best mentors you can have is an upperclassman that has taken the exact same path you are planning to take. They will guide you on exactly what to do from the resume and application process, to interviews, deadlines, and unwritten rules of conduct in the profession. The information is fresh and it will be detailed, so nothing gets better than this.

Mentors are there to bounce ideas off of. You might be faced with a situation that you have no idea how to handle. Mentors are there to guide you through it. You may be upset and frustrated over an incident, and in your youth and lack of experience could easily overreact or act in a manner that tarnishes your reputation and credibility. **Mentors are good at talking sense into you and making you look at the big picture.** Forget being politically correct; a good mentor will eventually develop the type of relationship with you where they can simply say, "Sharla, you should not wear that to work. It is inappropriate." **Valuable mentor relationships are built on honesty.**

Another thing to keep in mind is to never lose credibility with your mentor. Never discuss anything confidential your mentor shares with you to anyone else, and hopefully your mentor maintains that same level of confidentiality as well. You should try to develop the type of relationship where you can ask those questions you wouldn't feel comfortable asking someone else.

A professor can act as a mentor by providing you with invaluable information about your chosen career field. Also, they usually have inside connections to scholarships and various opportunities offered at the university that aren't necessarily public information.

With all of this wonderful support and guidance, one day I want you to become a mentor. You may feel that you may lack much real life experience in comparison to others, but guess what, you have lots to teach! **As doors are opened for you and new experiences are available to you, share that knowledge with someone else.**

# So what did you learn about mentoring relationships?

- No one in this world has become successful on their own.
- Mandatory mentors include:
  1) An upperclassman
  2) A professor or other faculty member
  3) Someone you admire and genuinely like
- Relationships are two-way streets.
- Schedule occasional meetings with your mentors to catch up on things.
- If your mentor offers you constructive feedback, don't go into a defensive mode.
- Whenever you see someone doing something positive, you can model that admirable quality.
- Mentors are good for talking sense into you and making you look at the big picture.
- Valuable mentor relationships are built on honesty.
- As doors are opened for you and new experiences are available to you, become a mentor and share that knowledge with someone else.

# Tip #10: Don't Be Too Hard On Yourself: Combat Feelings of Inferiority

During the teenage years and early twenties, most of you will think everything is a much bigger deal than it really is. In college, you will probably feel so passionately about certain things that you will be willing to start a revolution. If you break up with your boyfriend, five minutes later you are researching the process for joining a monastery. This is the time when you tend to take things way too far and usually blow things out of proportion.

Not knowing the proper way to react to these incidents makes sense. You are a rookie at this whole adult thing. College is a time of transition and this period can be challenging. You are simultaneously juggling your classes, maintaining a high GPA, choosing a major, building a resume, and developing your interview and networking skills. Then it's off to securing an internship and making a good impression, deciding whether to get a job or to go to graduate school, and the list goes on and on—but guess what? **College is a journey, a dynamic, fun-filled journey of growth and self-discovery. There are wonderful times and difficult times as well.**

I want you to remember that t**here are on-campus resources that are available for you.** One resource is your Resident Assistant. Hopefully you will have a really cool RA who you feel comfortable approaching about your particular issue. Let me dispel a myth once and for all about RAs: They are not the enemy! They are often perceived as the people that break up fun parties and report you to campus officials. If you don't feel comfortable approaching your RA, talk to someone else's RA, or bypass your RA and go to your RA's boss, usually called the Resident Director (RD). Your RA or RD can refer you to other resources on and off campus. On my campus, there was also a help line that students could call and anonymously receive advice. I'm sure your campus has similar services, but you must seek them out.

Next, there is another stereotype I need to nip in the bud: **People who see counselors are not crazy!** If most of the crazy people you see walking around the streets now had *free* resources, like an on-campus counseling center at their fingertips, they probably wouldn't be so "crazy" because they would receive help to get themselves through their tough situation. Sometimes it's nice to hear advice from an objective ear—someone who is not your best friend who knows all about you and may just brush off your feelings as if it's just another one of your crazy moments. **Counselors can give you an unbiased opinion and assessment.**

Friends, parents, and siblings can all be great resources as well. They know you well. Avoid those family members that brush your issues off whenever you call home, saying, "Oh that is just Brittany going through one of her dramatic moments again." That type of reaction never helps. Realize that the people close to you may not necessarily know how you feel.

You may get defensive when your family members give you advice. You may even stop listening even if the advice is good advice. Let's say your mom dropped out of college and when you call home to tell her about the D you just received on a test, she starts yelling at you. You're thinking, "Who the heck does she think she is, telling me I need to study more? She dropped out!" Well, she's giving you advice based on her own experiences. She dropped out and knows first hand about the repercussions of her decision. She probably regrets the decision she made and does not want to see you go down a similar path.

Always listen to the advice given, especially when it's from people that are genuinely concerned about you. Later on, you can filter through the advice and decide if you're actually going to use the advice or ignore it. But do listen to those with a good track record of loving and caring for you, like your parents and close family members. They've probably been where you are and just want the best for you.

As an RA during college, I amazingly escaped my two-and-a-half-year tenure without any attempted suicide calls, but I had plenty of co-RAs that averaged at least two a semester (and yes, there were calls from black girls). Usually a suicide threat is a cry for help. The hope I have for you is that you commit to getting yourself better by seeking help. Don't shut down the possibility of using campus resources. With things like group therapy sessions, which are oftentimes gender or race specific, it's amazing to discover how many people are struggling with the exact same issues you are facing.

Here are some common issues:

**1. You get a bad grade on an exam, fail a class, or get a low GPA for the semester and/or get on academic probation**

**"It is wise to keep in mind that no success or failure is necessarily final." -Unknown**

Any of the scenarios I listed above will get you down: you get a bad grade, you fail a class, or you get a low GPA for the semester. One thing I would advise you to do is to always **try your very best in everything that you do,** and you will minimize the regrets you have later on. You will minimize the "I wish I had studied" if you just study now. You will minimize the "I wish I had done the extra credit because then I would have gotten an A" by just doing the extra credit now so that you have a better chance of getting an A. Even if you study and do the extra credit and you still don't get the A, at least you know you tried your very best. Students usually know when a bad grade is coming. Do a self assessment. Did you really put in adequate study time? Remember that one or two bad exam grades will not make or break your semester or your life. Refer back to Tip # 3 and study daily! When your professor returns your exam, look at what you got wrong so that you will not make the same mistake again when it is time to take the final. Also, consider getting a tutor. Many on-campus tutoring services are offered free of charge. If you are on academic probation, you probably have one semester to bring your grades up or else you are withdrawn from the college. Ladies, it's time to get moving!

## 2. Blaming others for your failure

It is very easy to blame a friend or a guy you are in a relationship with for the C you received on your last exam. The mental replay goes something like this: "If I had not met Jerome, I would have a 4.0." "If Denise didn't drag me to the club every Thursday night, I would not be retaking this course." Guess what? **Everyone has choices.** Say no to Denise when she asks you to go out every Thursday night when you know you have a quiz every Friday. And yes, it's unfortunate you met Jerome when you did and you spent so much time together that it affected your grades, but since Jerome is no longer in the picture, let the studying begin! Keep in mind, blaming yourself is destructive as well. You may not have known any better at that time. Who knew partying would affect your grades the way that it did? You surely didn't. You saw everyone else doing it and thought you could pull it off as well. The good news is that now you know. **You must balance your time by making sure that your work gets done first and everything else gets done second.**

## 3. Being Embarrassed

It's easy to get caught up worrying and questioning what your peers think about you. Believe it or not, more than half the time they aren't even thinking about you at all! So what if you tripped in front of everyone at the step show? So what if you were in the talent show and got booed off stage? So what if you kissed one too many guys on your floor freshman year? No one is thinking about it half as much as you are. This is a perfect opportunity to withdraw and be reclusive, but there is no need to do that! The quicker you brush it off and move on with your life, the quicker you and everyone else forgets. I am not trying to minimize the actual embarrassment, but it is *not* the end of the world. This doesn't necessarily call for you to drop out of school or transfer. I can almost guarantee that people will soon forget what happened.

## 4. Constantly comparing yourself to others

Getting caught up in comparing yourself to others is self-defeating. You can go to your hometown and compare yourself to some of your peers in your neighborhood and think, "Wow, I'm doing great." Then you go back to school and compare your exam grade to a classmate's and then say, "Wow, I really need to step it up." College is filled with many smart students, and comparing yourself to others is always relative to the circumstances and people.

In certain areas of your life, you are on top of a mountain, meaning you are the best at what you do. Everything else is a little hill compared to you and your greatness. For example, in high school you could have been one of the most popular girls, captain of the cheerleading team, top ten percent of your class—I'm talking Miss Big Mountain here.

In college, the competition may get a bit tougher. All of a sudden you aren't Miss Big Mountain anymore. The small hills that once surrounded you all of a sudden appear much bigger. You have become a small hill. Once you enter a professional work environment or move into graduate school, your hill may become so small that you might forget you were ever a big mountain to begin with. Life (and moments when you feel less like a big mountain and more like a small hill) has a funny way of teaching you the concept of humility. No one will always be the tallest mountain in every aspect of life, every single time. Some aspects of your life will be mountains while other aspects will be small hills, but it's all relative. **Be grateful for your achievements** (or the big mountains in your life) and set goals to increase the size of your small hills in other areas of your life.

**Jealousy and envy can also be dangerous forces that are not just relevant in the college years.** If it is not who has the popular new love interest or the new car, later on in life it will be who has the bigger bank account, smarter children, or a better job. Comparisons in college can go beyond grades. Although you may not actually say it, you may be thinking, "I'm a little annoyed that Melissa got the internship I prepared so well for." "Charlene won the award, but I felt I deserved it more than she did!" "Arghhh! Lauren got the leadership position I wanted for so long." "Why is Jeanine so lucky in love? All the guys are so into her."

**Stretch yourself and attempt to be genuinely happy for the good that is happening in someone else's life.** It might just prompt you to get moving as well. Someone else's success can remind you of all the goals that you pushed to the wayside, but try not to get out of control and become vengeful, or even worse, beat yourself up mentally. These negative thoughts can be your worst enemy. Remain positive and focused on the future. Comparisons can be never-ending because there will always be people who are smarter, better looking, and richer than you are. Be content in whatever state you are in. Fully appreciate what you have.

## 5. Death of a loved one or another student

After my senior year of college, someone very close to me passed away. If you knew anything about our relationship, you would know that she was very special to me. She was my godmother, but also a friend and confidant. She died a slow death from cancer, and although I thought I was mentally prepared for her passing, that was far from the case. It hurt me deeply to know that I would never be able to spend time with her again. I wondered how I would ever be able to function without her, but despite the pain, I was able to handle it. From time to time I imagine her pushing me from behind, letting me know that things are going to be all right. **So despite the fact that this person will not be around physically, the person's presence will be with you and in your heart forever.**

There's no clear-cut way for me to tell you how to properly grieve. Grieving goes through several stages. The general stages are denial, anger, depression and acceptance. When my godmother passed, I decided to pretend as if she were still alive. That was a form of denial that obviously didn't work for more than a day. You may go through a period of anger, and blame others for this person's passing. You might think, "She would have lived longer if ..." You feel as if there is no way you can possibly live without this person in your life. You may become depressed and refuse to get close to anyone else again because the pain is too overwhelming when you lose them. Eventually you come to terms with their passing, and enter the stage of acceptance. I'm sure there are other possible stages of grief, but my point is that it's natural, so take your time to go through whatever stage you need to go through on your own. Grief is an individual experience. All I can recommend is that you reach out to family, friends, and campus resources. **Take all the time you need to be**

**alone and remember the happiest moments you had with your loved one.** Take a part of that person's spirit and let it guide you. You may not see it now, but there is a calm after the storm.

Throughout my four years in college, a handful of students died, and each death, whether or not I knew the student personally, was a slight blow to my heart. They were young and just beginning their lives, yet their life came to such a tragic end. During my senior year, three students that I knew died. One died of a brain aneurism, another died from alcohol poisoning, and the last student died in a house fire just weeks before graduation. During such a period of grief, the counseling center can be a primary resource. Reach out to other students and reflect on the positive moments you had with that person. You have a right to feel the uncertainty you may feel and have a right to deal with your experience the best way you can.

### 7. Homesickness

In the beginning of my freshman year, every month, without a doubt, you would find me on a bus to New Jersey. I was homesick! But the bus trips stopped in no time. **Once you begin to develop friendships and find your niche on campus, the trips home will become fewer and fewer.** Soon your parents will be begging you to visit at least once a semester. Adjusting to college may take time. It may take a semester or four to figure out where you belong, but like anything in life, you have to be patient. Take active steps by joining an organization or two and see what happens.

## 8. Transferring (after giving it one last chance)

Every student who goes to school away from home should return often enough to replenish themselves and to get a little at-home tender loving care. I think most students consider transferring a few times during their first year, usually after a not-so-pleasant experience. For example, you may go to a campus event and feel disconnected because of the magnitude of the student population, or it's been a few months and you still feel as if you don't belong.

If you realize a university is really not for you, by all means transfer to another school, especially for reasons like the school is too large and you feel like you are not getting the individual attention you need or it doesn't have the major in which you are interested. **Realize that it could be a case of homesickness.** Perhaps there are things you can do to feel more connected to your campus before you make the final decision to leave. The solution to your discomfort may rest in switching roommates, getting a lighter course load, switching your major, or finding a new extracurricular activity. Try an exchange program at another school for a semester if that option is available to you. If you know in your heart that it's really not the school for you, by all means transfer, but first talk to your advisor, a mentor, family, and upperclassmen. **In the end, it is really your call.** The best time to transfer is probably before the end of your freshman year, so the least damage is done credit-wise and you have time to acclimate successfully to another University.

Realize that even if you go to another school, work and studying still have to take place. You may face similar challenges, like forming friendships, especially now that you are no longer a brand-new student, but a transfer. You may also lose credit for courses you have completed.

> **Side Note #1:** Stay on top of the deadlines to apply to other schools, canceling your housing at your current school, and other mandatory deadlines at both schools.

## 9. Taking time off or dropping out

Many students decide to take time off for various reasons like money, family, personal issues, grades, a crisis, lack of focus, being burned out, or a host of other reasons. **Unfortunately, many people that do take time off never return.** If you can help it, do not take time off or drop out! The same advice I gave regarding a transfer is relevant here, reach out to as many resources as you can:

professors, counselors, and mentors. Oftentimes it just takes brainstorming and coming up with a plan to keep you in school.

I am aware that college is not for everyone and not everyone is mentally prepared for the demands of college. But keep in mind that after you take time to find yourself, nothing will change when you return. The work will still be there to be completed and if you have not taken any remedial actions during your time off (even if it's just a real self-assessment and analysis of your goals), you may come back to the same issues you were facing before you left. Before you know it, it becomes one year later and you have extended the degree earning process from a four-to-six-year plan into a seven-to-ten-year plan. This is a very expensive decision.

**During your time off, rethink you goals and come back when you are ready to devote your time and focus to being a student.** The longer you are out of school, the more difficult it is for you to return. If you realize college is not for you and you decide to completely drop out and not come back, I hope you have *really* thought about your decision, talked to plenty of people, and have a plan B ready for action.

**Side Note #2:** The student loan people will be after you in about six months to begin repaying your loans. I hope you have a good job. They will find you. And if you think you can avoid paying them, they will begin taking the money you owe them directly out of your paycheck.

## 10. Other Coping Strategies: Religion

I've already mentioned counseling, of which I am a huge fan. Another resource is your faith. Perhaps for most of you, this is your first resource. No matter what your belief is and whoever your God is, reach out to Him. Individuals and situations will let you down, but your higher connection will not. There are on-campus resources like the campus church and chapel or local houses of worship in the surrounding community if you want to pray in a fellowship with others. It is wonderful when you find a church home away from home. Explore different churches until you find a good fit. Do keep one very important thing in mind: **Faith without work is dead.** In other words, while you are praying for God to help you pass your chemistry exam, you should also be putting in work by studying.

## 11. Not being able to afford school

College can be very expensive, but there are more ways to afford it than most people think. Financial aid uncludes grants, scholarships, work study, and loans. Grants are given based on your financial need and do not have to ever be repaid (e.g., The Pell Grant). Scholarships are awarded for strong academic achievement, a particular talent/skill, financial need, or a combination of academic achievement and financial need. Work study is earned by working part-time. Loans must be repaid on a monthly basis once you are no longer a full-time student (e.g., Stafford Loan).

If you come from a low-income household, you can be awarded need-based financial aid. Every student must begin by filling out the FAFSA (Free Application for Federal Student Aid) in order to just be eligible to receive financial aid from the government. It's important to complete your FAFSA as soon as possible after January 1st preceding the academic year you need aid because aid is given on a first come basis! Additionally, colleges usually award aid as well, so be sure to discuss this with your admissions counselor.

The financial aid package you receive is based on the information you reported in your FAFSA. The government will determine how much your family is able to contribute to funding your education. You may get, for example, a certain amount of grants and eligibility for loans and work study. When your total aid does not cover your entire cost to attend college, you will have to come up with the rest of the money.

The beauty of scholarships is that there are a plethora of them out there. Scholarships are awarded by your college, major corporations and institutions, churches, clubs, and individuals. Additionally, many scholarships are minority based. The unfortunate element to scholarships is that usually the same top performers who apply, win the scholarships, whether academic, athletic, or based on a unique quality. Your job is to become a top performer! A major element of winning scholarships is your GPA; that is why you must study daily and maintain a high GPA from the start. Also, scholarship success is often times a numbers game. Write a really good generic essay that you can tweak for various scholarships depending on the essay question. Make several copies of your essay. Ask the person writing your recommendation to make several copies and provide them stamped and addressed envelopes for them to mail their recommendation. Then fill out the applications and apply to every single scholarship for which you qualify! You already have copies of the essay and recommendation, so the rest of the application should be fairly easy.

You can find scholarships in your major through Internet searches and campus postings, and even closer and more accessible are the scholarships offered at your school. Don't be turned off by scholarships that require a writing piece. Usually college students are too lazy to write the essay and end up missing out on tons of money. That lessens the candidate pool and increases your chances of winning. Consider applying for scholarships sponsored by your church or asking for a donation.

**Visit your campus financial aid office** if you have not already done so. There is financial aid out there! If you have to, get a part-time job. You can become a Resident Assistant and have your room and board waived. You may consider going to a community college for a semester or two to cut costs. Just make sure that the credits from your community college transfer over to your main university.

## 12. Rape

Your body is a temple, and no one has the right to touch you in a manner that you have not provided consent. Rape is a very common occurrence in college. Oftentimes alcohol is involved and you know who the perpetrator is. Whether alcohol is involved or not, when you know the perpetrator who committed the rape, it is called "date rape." You must be conscious and in control at all times, primarily in risky environments like a party where alcohol is involved. Have friends around that can be designated to not drink that night and will intervene when your behavior gets out of control. **No means no, and if you are forced to do something you did not consent to, report the event to the police and see someone in the counseling center.** You cannot allow this person to get away with violating your body, nor can you allow this to potentially happen to someone else. You are not dirty or unworthy and it is not your fault.

**Side Note #3:** Be conscious of walking around campus alone late at night. Use the campus escort or transportation services.

## 13. Pregnancy

Whether you are in a monogamous relationship or not, you should always protect yourself while having sex, from sexually transmitted diseases and pregnancy. College is a popular time for girls to get pregnant, particularly senior year. If you are already pregnant, no one can tell you what to do with your pregnancy—whether to keep the child, have an abortion, or give your child up for adoption.

Every child is a blessing. If you have a child, hopefully you will still be able to finish school. The thousands of mothers that finish school while having a young child to take care of at home should be saluted! Being a mother is one of the most important jobs you will ever have in your life. You want to be in the position to adequately provide for a child. For many students, the college years are not the most ideal time. You are very young, probably not married, and probably cannot financially provide for a child. **If you are going to have sex, protect yourself** so that you are able to finish school and adequately provide for a child.

**Side Note #4:** Remember that whomever you have sex with is a potential father of your child.

Now that I've gone through thirteen issues you may potentially face, remember that life consists of many highs, lows, and in-betweens, similar to the ebb and flow of an ocean. It is the humility that you gain during the lows and in-betweens that often gives you the drive to pursue more highs. **Your goal should be to reach a state of *inner peace*. Perhaps start writing in a journal**. Remember that everything that you are going through is just a small part of your life, a mere millionth of the total equation of your life. There is much more in store for you.

## Combat feelings of Inferiority: Adversity=Growth

Each one of us has a story. It is the fine details of your individual story that shapes your character and makes you the individual you are today. A great deal of your character is shaped from childhood experiences. Since the college years are defining years in which you mold and shape your identity, many unsettled issues that have been suppressed all of your life finally come to light. Your family makeup has a great deal to do with who you are.

Some of you grew up with maids and nannies and lived like the Huxtables (*The Cosby Show* family that is considered the ideal black family). Others grew up with parents that were in and out of jail, addicted to drugs, or struggled to work two or three jobs to put food on the table. Some of you grew up with fathers; some of you did not. Some of you grew up being the shining stars in your family, with constant praise and a multitude of opportunities. Others grew up feeling inadequate, with constant criticism and abuse directed toward them or other family members. Some of you went on family vacations every summer; others have never been outside their states' borders. Some of you were introduced to calamari and wine by age ten, while others are still trying to figure out what exactly calamari is. No matter where you started out or what happened in your past, the potential of your life is so much more.

In addition to your childhood, you may have also endured some more recent circumstances that caused you to feel doubtful, inadequate, or unworthy. It may be a relationship that you put so much time and effort into only to find out it was built on lies. It could be a constant pursuit of an internship or job and all you have been met with is rejection. Or it could be after you secure an internship or a job and you find out all the other interns attend an Ivy League school and you attend a college no one in the world has ever heard of. Or it could be a brush with racism or sexism that seems to alter your view of the world. You begin to question your competence and second guess your abilities and if you actually deserve to be where you are. *Do I deserve this opportunity? Am I smart enough?*

I am here to tell you that **you are not inferior and you deserve all of the blessings that come your way. Whatever you have been through is maturing you to a place of clarity and understanding about life, and your purpose here on earth.** And little do you know, your peers are having the same mental dialogue with themselves and feeling the same exact insecurities. It's really not a question of if you will have these moments of doubt and vulnerability in your life; it's more a question of what you are going to do when these moments hit you. The period that is most important is after your last low. What are you going to do to motivate yourself to get back in action? Let's say you just realized you have no idea how you are going to afford the next semester of school. You have two options: sulk, cry, and lock yourself in your room for two weeks; or you can get on your grind and talk to everyone you know in the financial aid office, apply for scholarships, talk to family members and mentors that might be able to assist you financially, and contact your bank for a loan. **Do not wallow in your own self-pity.**

## Racism

So you all know that racism exists, and if you have never experienced it before there is a very high and likely chance you will experience it in college, whether it be on campus, during an internship, or even walking around the surrounding community. If it were still up to some people, you would not be in college right now. It is unfortunate that people still have these negative thoughts, but sadly they do. Once you are hit with a dose of racism you may question if all attacks or questions of your character are cases of racism. You may even begin to question whether you can trust some racial groups as a whole.

The first experience that made me question if racism occurred was during one of the four internships I had. During a training session, one of my fellow white male intern "friends" refused to call me by my name. He referred to me as "that girl" even though we sat at the same table next to each other for two weeks and for at least eight hours per day. The worst thing is that to this day he probably doesn't even realize that he did what he did and that it was offensive to me. Although I was offended, I had to take the responsibility of thinking through that situation. Was that exactly racism or that individual's ignorance? I definitely believe it was the latter. I can't make such a broad judgment of a race of people based on my negative interactions with one person. Sometimes people will offend you and that person may have no clue that they did anything offensive. For two weeks, everyone else called me by my name. He decided I was "that girl." Initially I was angry. It was a huge deal to me. How could I be sitting right next to him and yet he continued to ignore my presence? Eventually I had to move on.

My second brush with racism occurred when I was driving home from a get-together in Baltimore, Maryland. I was with two female friends and we were lost, so I pulled up next to two white males and said, "Excuse me," several times. I was no more than two feet away from them. I continued to say, "Excuse me," while I honked my horn insistently. Their windows were down, so I knew they heard me, but they kept their heads turned forward and did not look in my direction. How could I be within reaching distance to them and they ignore me like that?

Today, in a more mature frame of mind, when I think of my two experiences, they were absolutely nothing compared to what others experience daily, but at that time it was a big deal because I had never experienced anything like that in my entire life. Maybe neither experience had to do with race. Perhaps the guy in my training class was a jerk and would have been a jerk if I was black, blue, or purple. Perhaps the second group of men that refused to acknowledge me had been attacked previously and refused to risk it. Whether it was racism or not, **I cannot allow these events to hinder me from being the best I can be and reaching my fullest potential.** What am I willing to lose sleep over? I have to choose my battles.

**Don't give a person or a group of people that much power over your life and don't let some one else's insecurities stop you from being the best you can be.** There may be hate crimes on your campus and other racially charged events. You can do your part to fight the issue, but realize that racism and discrimination may never go away so you can not let it prevent you from fulfilling your dreams.

**Side Note #5: Just because you have been hurt or slighted by one, two, or even ten racist individuals, remember that is who they are.** They do not represent an entire race of people.

If you need to vent, try a dialogue group. These groups allow students to discuss controversial topics, such as race, in a facilitated environment. Sometimes individuals of a certain race may not understand your side and you may not understand their perspective either. Stereotypes and generalizations can easily be interpreted as facts. Once you engage in a dialogue, at least you will understand someone else's perspective.

You have two choices in tough situations having to do with race: You can react or let it go. Sometimes it is hard to let it go if you feel slighted or disrespected. Usually you have to say something. But before you do, **think things over: Take a deep breath, and then react if you are so inclined.** Also, sometimes your most explosive and instantaneous reactions are the most inappropriate and lead to the most severe repercussions. Colin Powell once said, "Let [racism] be a problem to someone else. Let it drag them down. Don't use it as an excuse for your own shortcomings."

Commit to the continuous process of positive thinking and putting things into perspective. Do what it takes: read self-help books, say daily affirmations, and listen to inspirational messages on your ipod. Train your mind to control your thoughts. Don't ever believe you are not good enough. Be confident in yourself and your abilities, and most importantly, love yourself!

## So what did you learn about being hard on yourself and combating feelings of inferiority?

- College is a journey.
- There are resources out there that are available to you.
- People who see counselors are *not* crazy.
- Sometimes it helps to talk to someone who doesn't know you. They can give you an objective opinion and assessment.
- Try your best in everything that you do to avoid regrets later on.
- Everyone has choices. Try not to blame others for your failure.
- You must balance your time by making sure your work gets done first and everything else gets done second.
- Be grateful for your achievements.
- Jealousy and envy can be dangerous forces that are not just relevant in the college years.
- Stretch yourself and attempt to be genuinely happy for someone else.
- If someone dies, despite the fact that this person will not be around physically, the person's presence will be with you and in your heart forever. Reach out to family, friends, and campus resources. Take all the time you need to be alone and remember the happiest moments you had with your loved one.

- If you are feeling homesick, know that adjusting takes time. Once you find your niche on campus you will be going home less often.
- If you feel you want to transfer, realize that it could be a case of homesickness. Talk to people before making that final decision to transfer.
- Most people that take time off never return to school, so avoid this at all costs.
- If you take time off, be sure to rethink your goals and come back to school when you are ready to devote your time and focus to being a student.
- Faith without work is dead. As you are praying for God to help you pass your chemistry exam, you should also be studying.
- Visit your campus financial aid office.
- No means no, and if you are forced to do anything physical and you did not provide consent, report the event to the police and see someone in the counseling center.
- Protect yourself from sexually transmitted diseases and pregnancy.
- Your goal should be a feeling of *inner peace*. Start writing in a journal.
- You are *not* inferior!
- Whatever you have been through is maturing you to a place of clarity and understanding about life and your purpose.
- You cannot allow racist actions to hinder you from being the best you can be and reaching your fullest potential.

- Don't give a person or a group of people that much say in your life, and don't let someone else's insecurities stop you from being the best you can be.
- Just because you have been hurt or slighted by one, two, or even ten racist individuals, remember that is who they are.
- When you encounter racism, think things over; take a deep breath and then react, because it may not be as big of a deal as you initially thought. Also, sometimes your most explosive and instantaneous reactions are the most inappropriate.

# Tip #11: Achieve Balance: The Juggling Act

Think of yourself now as an amateur juggler. Your goal in this circus called college is to juggle what seems like a million balls at once. These balls translate into a million different commitments, both personal and academic. This includes balancing time, money, food, exercise, and your mental and physical health. **Time management can become a game of trial and error until you figure out what really works for you.**

Here's one example of a perfect juggling act:

| | |
|---|---|
| Sleeping | 7 hrs |
| Eating | 2.25 hrs |
| Classes | 3.75 hrs |
| Gym/Favorite Show or Two | 2 hrs |
| E-mail/ Instant Messenger/Facebook/MySpace | 2 hrs |
| Studying | 7 hrs |
| Total Hours | 24 hrs |

Some of the balls that must be juggled include:

**1) Studying: You should allocate several hours in your day for focused study.** See Tip #3 and study daily!

**2) Your Health: Take your vitamins, eat properly, get enough sleep, and work out**! Freshman fifteen, twenty, and thirty are real. It is very easy to gain weight in college. **Your goal should be to make exercise a part of your daily schedule.** It really does not matter if you have been relatively petite your entire life. College brings so many weight-gaining factors into your life, like late-night junk eating, alcohol (if you drink), a much more sedentary lifestyle if you were active in high school, and an erratic sleep schedule. After you gain the freshman fifteen, it's not as if the fifteen pounds immediately melt away at the end of your freshman year. After you've gained freshman fifteen, you might also fall victim to sophomore fifteen, junior fifteen, and potentially senior fifteen if you do not get a grip on managing your weight. Get moving ladies!

**Develop an exercise plan early on.** Try classes at the gym and make exercise a priority. There are no pills, gizmos, or gadgets that is going to whittle your waistline, so aim for at least thirty minutes of daily activity.

> **Side Note #1:** Exercise has been proven to improve your mood. If you find yourself slipping into a funk, hit the treadmill!

**Side Note #2:** Try to minimize the length of your daily naps, or you could end up sleeping away entire days at a time.

Making the healthiest choices when it comes to food is important. I usually ran out of money on my food plan at the end of the semester, which forced me to go out and purchase more off-campus food, and I am not talking about fruits and vegetables here. I'm talking more like pizza, Chinese food, buffalo wings, and sandwiches. Most campuses have a variety of food. Some of it is good for you, and some can be loaded with fat and calories, but you always have an option to eat the calorie-laden foods or the healthier options. The convenience of an on-campus meal plan is that when you are ready to eat, the food is available. You don't have to go and prepare anything. If you don't mind going to the grocery store and cooking, and you actually have a kitchen, not having a meal plan is the best choice for you. If you live on campus, most traditional halls do not have the option for residents to cook. You may have to wait until you are an upperclassman or move off campus to a place with a stove before you can begin cooking for yourself.

You should focus on eating a good balance of food, including carbohydrates. Be sure to include fresh fruits and vegetables in your daily diet. An unbalanced diet will not only add those unwanted pounds, they will also contribute to a lack of energy. Remember that fresh food is always better than processed food. Also, the dining hall sometimes gives huge portions of the bad stuff and limits their portion of the good stuff. It is okay to eat half of the giant size serving of pasta. Pre-plan what you're going to eat. Campus food can also be bland, so figure out how to add the right hot sauce or whatever it takes to get the taste just right. Avoid excessive late-night eating. You will probably gain weight and people will have their comments and reactions when you get home. Try not to let that get to you.

**Side Note #3: Black people get eating disorders too**. Black people get the same eating disorders you think are only in the movies. Anorexia and bulimia can happen to anyone. Or you can develop disordered eating habits where you gain and lose excessive amounts of weight in short time frames. You may never go to the doctor to actually get diagnosed, but this is not healthy either. If you realize you are having issues striking a healthy balanced diet, seek help from a campus nutritionist that can help you create a well-balanced health regimen.

You must also learn to manage your schedule so that you plan your assignments and exams to ensure you are not overly committed and overly stressed. Too many commitments equal stress, which equals inadequate sleep, which usually leads to poor eating and no exercise, which all makes you more susceptible to irritability and illness. For example, if you have a paper to complete, set a deadline for research, a deadline for your first draft, and another deadline for your final draft.

**Beware of germy sicknesses that are prevalent in college settings.** There is a popular flu-like sickness in college that spreads around freshman dorms like the plague; it's called "mono." Mono it short for "infectious mononucleosis." It is also known as "the kissing disease." And the worst part is that you can get it whether you actually kiss someone or not. I'm not going to get into the gory details, but just be careful when you are around sick people. Also be conscious of things like sharing drinks and straws. Schedule a regular checkup at the health center, and if you are sick, be sure to go and see the doctor.

Now beyond those minor illnesses, there are viruses and diseases of a much more serious nature. **STDs are real.** Whether or not you feel an itch, twitch, or burn, you should get yourself checked out on a regular basis, especially if you are sexually active. Furthermore, you should not be engaging in sexual activities without protection. The result of not protecting yourself is the possibility of various sexually transmitted diseases and pregnancy. Even if you are in a monogamous relationship, you should never be so convinced your boyfriend will not have sex with someone else. A curable STD might seem okay and livable, but there are things that don't go away, like herpes or genital warts (HPV), and even worse, HIV and AIDS. Also, when you have unprotected sex with someone, you are not just having sex with them. You are having sex with all the people they had sex with and all the additional people those people had sex with and the list goes on and on till you've essentially had sex with so many people you can't even count. Schedule STD exams at least annually and when you change sexual partners. Make sure you are also tested for HIV/AIDS. It is quite alarming to know that African-American women in their early-to mid-twenties are the fastest growing population of HIV/AIDS cases! *Please* protect yourself!

**Side Note #4:** Why not schedule an appointment for you and your boyfriend to get tested for HIV together?

**Smoking:** Lots of people smoke in college and you may become one of them, but when you really think about it, it makes absolutely no sense. Cigarettes are expensive and you don't have money to waste. Cigarettes cause lung cancer and premature lines and wrinkles. I know that you've probably heard that *black don't crack*, but add cigarettes to the equation and you will definitely age yourself prematurely. So what are the benefits again? Now let's switch gears to smoking that "other stuff." That "other stuff" is illegal, so let's not even go there. You were raised better than that. You can get kicked off campus and face criminal penalties for this offense. It's so not worth it when succeeding in college is your number one priority.

**Be sure to schedule activities that you enjoy and put you at peace,** whether that means watching your favorite show daily, attending a yoga class, or going to see a movie. Enjoy these activities for your mental health and well-being.

**3) Money:** Unless you come from a wealthy home where you have access to as much cash as you want, you receive a really nice financial aid refund check, or you have a very well-paying job, you *will* be broke in college. Although the majority of students are broke, you do develop a skill in finding creative ways to make your dollar stretch. If you listened to my advice from "The First Days" chapter, hopefully you have stayed far away from those credit card people and are not in credit card debt.

If you fell into temptation, I want you to **commit to at least paying the minimum *on time* on a monthly basis.** This means mailing in the payment at least one week in advance of the due date. Even better, you can make your payment online to avoid any late penalties or fees. Credit card debt is a nightmare and you do not want it. Pay off your debt as fast as you can and learn from your mistake.

Take control of your spending. One way to do this is to create a budget and stick to it. You can also cut costs in other ways. For example, head straight for the sales rack when you go shopping and limit off-campus eating to the weekends only. Remember that small things add up to big things. A lot of students' downfall is caffeine. If you spend too much money on cappuccinos or iced lattes, it will deplete your savings and add a few inches to your waistline as well.

**Side Note #5: Be sure to save your money from summer jobs and internships.** You are usually making significantly more than you make with a campus job, especially if your summer employment is a well-paid internship. Get into the habit of saving now.

**Side Note #6:** There are so many free activities on campus and students usually don't take full advantage of them. In addition to your tuition, you pay a student activities fee that covers these free campus events. Don't let this money go down the drain. Save some of the money you are spending going out each weekend.

**Side Note #7:** For many of you who are going to school and have student loans and grants that are not covering the entire cost of your education, there might be someone working very long hours, perhaps two or three jobs for you to attend school. This could be your mother, father, grandmother, or another adult. Think about it: Someone is making a huge sacrifice for your future. If you take your education as a joke, you will lose this luxury in an instant. Parents usually have a very low tolerance for their money being wasted. There are no do over's in school and in life. The poor choices you make now in balancing your time and keeping your grades up will impact you for the rest of your life, and in so many ways that are not evident to you right now.

**4) Household chores:** Laundry definitely tends to pile up if a routine is not established, especially since you usually have to lug your laundry to another location in your building or on campus. The weekends can be chaotic, so **try to do your laundry in the middle of the week and monitor the time it's in the machine**. Students will take your laundry out and put it wherever they feel like it! That is when you start losing socks here and there. Try studying nearby while you wait for your laundry in the washer and dryer.

> **Side Note #8:** Save your quarters! It sucks when the change machine is broken and you still have a load of wet clothes that need to be dried. Another option for those that live close to home is to bring your laundry home to wash for free, or you might even be able to convince your mom or dad to do it for you!

> **Side Note #9:** Try to **keep your room organized.** This helps when you are studying or packing, and it develops good skills for later

on in your life. Keep important documents, like your financial aid documents, in a safe place.

**Side Note #10:** Develop a schedule with those you are living with for trash and common area cleaning. A cleaning routine is best if it is established earlier on than later.

**5) Jobs/Sports:** I understand that many of you will have to fund a portion if not all of your tuition, books, or room and board with a side job or athletic scholarship.

**Side Note #11:** Be sure to reflect your financial contribution toward your college education on your resume. For example, "Funded 100 percent of education by working forty-plus hours weekly."

I would advise you to **keep your commitment to work at a minimum, meaning less than twenty hours a week.** If you *must* work (meaning you have many unavoidable bills to pay, i.e. you are not working just for a fresh pair of boots every month), explain to your employer that you are a full-time college student and ask if they are okay with this and if they will be flexible with emergency situations, such as group meetings or a tutorial session. Be a good worker because if you are a slacker, your supervisor will be less inclined to allow you to take time off from work for a school related project.

If you are an athlete, and particularly if you are on a scholarship, your schedule is pretty much regimented by the athletic program. You have less control over your overall schedule. However, if you feel you are falling behind on your studies because of your commitment to sports, speak with your coach. Perhaps they can work out an arrangement for you. If you are playing a sport, and not on a scholarship, (and the likelihood of you becoming a professional athlete is unlikely), you may consider quitting the team; especially if your academics are suffering.

Take an internship during the semester if you are close to graduation and have had no significant internships. Limit your commitment outside of your internship and classes. Don't be the president of anything. Have a light course load that semester. The two semesters when I had internships were very stressful. I also had two leadership positions on campus at the same time. You are too young to be stressed and you have the rest of your life to work a forty-plus hour work week.

If you would like a little extra cash, as *everyone* does in college, I would recommend an on-campus job. Although these jobs are usually low paying, it is very convenient to be able to walk to work, or in situations when you have to explain to your supervisor that you have a huge exam the next day. My best job was at the front desk of an information center. People came by to ask questions, but in-between asking questions, guess what I was doing? That's right, ladies; I was studying. I chose to work one really early morning shift: seven a.m. to noon. Sounds long and inconvenient, but it was one of the best decisions I ever made. Hardly any one came to the desk during those early morning hours and that is when I got the most work done. Similar jobs would be at the campus library or a ticket office.

6) **Your Ambition:** Now is the time to be gutsy! Study in England for a semester, accept that fall semester co-op in NY, accept the summer internship in Ohio, but you don't want to fall victim to the *Superwoman Syndrome* I referenced in Tip # 5 "Get Involved Early On." Identify when you are wearing yourself too thin.

> **Side Note #12:** Once you begin conquering the world, you may begin to feel as though you have a great deal of valuable information to share with others and begin to mind other people's business. Important point: **mind your business!**

> **Side Note #13:** I also notice that many students have a sense of entitlement after a series of wonderful things come their way. You are not entitled to anything in life. Remain humble and be grateful that you have worked hard and are extremely blessed.

7) **Important Dates/Deadlines: Write down important dates** in the planner you picked up from the bookstore in "The First Days." For example, you need to write

down when you need to complete your Free Application for Federal Student Aid (FAFSA). Again, the FAFSA is the application to be completed annually in order to qualify for all types of financial aid for college. The form is distributed and processed by the United States Department of Education. Without your FAFSA, you can say good-bye to your loans, grants, and work-study.

Use your planner to plan your weeks ahead of time. This will allow you to schedule the incremental steps for a big assignment. When you plan your weeks, be sure to include time for exercise and enjoyable activities. Most important, remember to factor in study time!

Write down when you need to meet with your advisor to discuss the classes you must take each semester. This will ensure you are on the right track to fulfill all of your course requirements to graduate on time.

> **Side Note #14:** Be aware of the classes that are only held during one semester of the academic year, so you can plan your schedule accordingly. For example, a particular course may only be held in the fall and not in the spring. Remember, your first semester should be limited to twelve to fifteen credits only. Take a summer class or two if you think you will fall behind schedule for graduation.

**Taxes:** The tax filing deadline (April 15th) applies to you too. You have to file taxes annually. If you are in school out of state, you have to fill out a non-resident form and file in your home state, unless you have established residency in the new state. More likely than not, your parents will be claiming you as a dependent. Most scholarships are non-taxable.

> **Side Note #15:** There are also tax credits that can be claimed by you or your parents depending on how you choose to file. The Hope Tax Credit is a tax credit applied during the first two years of college and the lifetime learning credit may be claimed annually. You cannot claim both credits for the same student in the same year, but your parents can use one credit for one student in college and another credit for another student. Your parents can use the Hope credit during your freshman and sophomore year, and then the lifetime learning credit during your junior and senior year. Additionally, there are various college savings programs you should inquire about with your family's accountant.

8) **Classes and Scheduling:** Use the scheduling resources available to you, such as an online schedule of classes. Have several options available as a second or third choice in case you do not get into the class you want. See what classes require a prerequisite course. You my have to take another class and pass successfully before you are eligible to take the next class. Also read reviews of professors if they are available.

Do not just choose the professors that will give you an easy A. You may actually want to learn something!

But if it's a class you know you are weak in and it has nothing to do with your major, get that easy professor before everyone else does!

If you are registering and a class is full, go and talk to the professor or call the registration office and express how badly you want to get into this class. You can also attend the first class and talk to the professor about your situation. Add yourself to the waiting list and check it frequently.

Take a one credit gym class, study skills class, or another easy class to balance out a tough semester, but **don't try to overkill your schedule with electives and procrastinate taking your major courses.**

Diversify your electives. For example, if your schedule permits, take a few business classes. Despite your major and future job position, many of you will end up working in a for profit establishment, so it's good to get a general understanding of business. Also, you may have some entrepreneurial side ventures you want to explore later on in life. Knowing a bit about business won't hurt. Likewise, business majors should take a few classes unrelated to business. No one should leave their university without taking a black cultural studies course.

Before you schedule, talk to people! Speak to your peers in your major, and upperclassmen as well. Keep in mind that not all advice is good advice, so consider the source. Someone convinced me to take a particular course for an easy A. It was one of the most annoying classes I took because I had absolutely no interest in the subject.

**Take classes at times that fit into your lifestyle.** I do not suggest eight a.m. classes, unless it's a great professor, you're a morning person, and that is the only timeslot available. Remember to try to schedule your classes as soon as you can, add yourself to the wait list if need be, and check the wait list frequently. Read the schedule of classes and decide what the best time of day is for you to take a class. Is it better for you to take the course at ten a.m. or two p.m.? Again, I personally would stay away from either end of the spectrum. Eight a.m. classes are tough to wake up for and by the evening hours your concentration may not be there fully for an evening course. Huge breaks in between classes aren't good either. For example, having an eight a.m. class and then not having another class until four p.m. isn't good. You want enough of a break to have lunch or take an occasional nap, but if the break is too long you may be less inclined to return back to campus for class. Also, scheduling your classes together allows a better timeframe for working if you decide to get a part-time job. Avoid Friday classes if you can!

**Side Note #15:** Get to know a few people in Administration for scheduling, registering, and financial issues.

9) **Midterms and Finals:** During midterms and finals, all of your exams are within the same time frame, which can equate to stress, stress, and more stress. Keeping up throughout the semester helps a great deal, especially when it's a cumulative final. This means you are being tested on *everything* you've learned during the semester. Refer back to Tip #3 "Study Daily" for study techniques. Be sure to break up your studying into more manageable parts.

**All-nighters:** I've mentioned this before: pull all-nighters if you have to. The better tactic is to study daily and keep up with material. It is important to be well rested before an exam; however, if you have not studied at all for an exam, being well rested with no information in your brain doesn't help you get a decent grade. Get your caffeine and a healthy snack and go study!

**Cheating/Plagiarism: Don't do it. Case closed.** You can get expelled or there may be a permanent mark on your transcript that anyone requesting your transcript will be able to see. Employers do not want to be associated with individuals with unethical tendencies. Give others credit for their words and ideas. Include a "Works Cited" page when you make specific references to their text.

**10) Your Safety and Security:** Crime is a reality on all college campuses. If you go to a large university with an open campus, it is extremely difficult to prevent outsiders from coming onto campus and committing crimes. Your fellow schoolmates can be perpetrators of robberies, muggings, and rape as well. Do not let your guard down with protecting yourself. **Do not take nightly strolls on campus alone.** Be conscious of the safety lights and call boxes your school has put into place for your safety. Lock your bedroom/suite door before going to sleep. Use on-campus security personnel, particularly if your campus has an escort service or transportation system for late-night travel.

> **Side Note #16:** Purchase a landline phone (a phone that is not a cordless) so that in case there is a power outage you can make an emergency phone call.

**11) Having Fun:** Refer to Tip #1 "Have Fun." **Go on a spring break trip every year that you can afford it** (not when your credit card can afford it—when *you* can afford it)!

Beware of spring break package scams. These scam artists usually set up shop only during spring break, take hundreds of students' dollars, and only deliver on half of what they promise. Try to find a reputable company from a friend that used the agency to book one of his or her spring break trips in the past. Also, never vacation with people who easily annoy you or aren't down for things you are down with. Vacations are supposed to be fun. No one wants to go anywhere with someone who is always in the hotel room not wanting to do anything! Go to spring break spots like Cancun, Jamaica, Miami—places where you know spring-breakers will be. Go with a responsible group and be careful when you're there.

Can't afford spring break? Take road trips to visit other surrounding schools for their events and visit some of the colleges and universities in which your high school friends are currently enrolled. Sign up for an alternative spring break where you do a community service activity during that particular week.

**Partying:** There might be kegs, people playing beer pong, or students just drinking and having a good time. College is great for the independence you have, but this freedom requires a great deal of responsibility. **Bring along a friend or two to the parties, especially when alcohol is involved.** Alcohol can make the most church-going usher into a frolicking fool. When you lose control of your inhibitions you can end up being raped. Someone can slip a type of poisoning in your drink called rohyprol, which gets you extra intoxicated. This allows a person to take full advantage of you. You will barely remember it the next day. You can end up in a fight, arrested, and/or physically injured in more ways than you can imagine.

**Side Note #17:** If a party is in a dorm room, be aware that you may get in trouble if you are caught at the party, especially if you are an underage drinker. This applies to off-campus parties as well. Surrounding residents usually end up calling the police for the loud noise. Have a clear path to the nearest exit.

**Drunkenness:** If you have the pleasure of turning twenty-one in college (or managed to acquire a fake id, which is illegal, as you know) you know all too well about drinking and partying. On my campus there were several bars that were in walking distance. Everyone went to these hot spots on Thursday nights to get $1 drinks. With alcohol in your system, you say and do the things that you may regret later on.

You want to assign one person in your friendship group who will not drink and will be the designated driver or designated responsible person so that when it is time to go home, she can help escort you back to campus. Make sure you and your friends make an agreement with each other that you will watch over each other in the event you start kissing all the boys in the club and/or you begin to create a really bad reputation for yourself.

**Side Note #18:** After consecutive nights of partying and drinking your skin may become flushed from the dehydrating effects of alcohol, and over time you develop that not so sexy beer belly. **Remember: Study and do your work before you party.**

**Side Note #19:** Overindulgence in college will mess you up. It could be overdosing on partying, overdosing on food, or overdosing on not studying. Overindulgence will have you headed in the direction of failure.

12) **Moving Off Campus (*only* after your freshman year, preferably after sophomore year):** Roommates and dorm rules can become a drag if the RA is anal and your roommate has issues, but realize that everyone is going through a similar situation. **If you are going to live off campus, live within walking distance to campus or within walking distance to public transportation** if you do not have a car, or for days when you do not want to drive to campus even if you do have a car.

Be cautious of living with your closest friends. Oftentimes this living situation does not work out and you end up losing a close friend in the end. No matter who you live with, make sure you have similar or tolerable lifestyles.

I think all students should aim to live on campus their first year. By not living on campus, you will miss out on some of the best friendship building opportunities. After a while, the constant moving in and out every year does become annoying. Renting an apartment is better in this regard, but if you are going to go home for the summer or have internships in other states, you'll usually have to sublease your space. Finding someone to rent can be a hassle.

I've seen some students move off campus, and improve their grades, but I've seen it prove to be disastrous for many. It all depends on the type of student you are and your study habits. Moving off campus makes it that much easier to oversleep and decide it would be pointless to rush and try to make it to your class on time, especially if there is heavy traffic to your university and you have to find parking. If you are disciplined enough to do that, then that's great. Moving off campus can work for you.

While on-campus dining is not the most appetizing, it sure saves a great deal of time if you do not have to cook. If you enjoy cooking, living somewhere with a kitchen can be a better arrangement and can probably be an improvement to your overall diet. If you don't have a car or a reliable mode of transportation, I would advise staying on campus until you do. Having a car is almost essential, not only for getting to and from classes, but also for last minute runs to campus for group meetings, or for trips to the supermarket. Be conscious of the expenses you will incur once you move off campus, such as utilities, food, cable, and an Internet connection. When you live on campus, these bills are packaged together as an overall fee.

**Side Note #20:** You can store some of your large items you don't want to lug back home in summer storage for a fee. Oftentimes, storage companies advertise on campus right around the end of each semester. If not, check with your RA for information on these resources.

**Side Note #21:** Avoid shacking up with your boyfriend in college. You will have plenty of time for that later on, if you so desire. Avoid joint credit cards, apartment, or any other financial ties.

13) A Car: With a car comes expenses such as maintenance, a possible car note, an annual permit fee, tires, breaks, oil changes, insurance, and other expenses, which will cost you more money than you may have planned. Once I got a car, I also began to spend more money because I was able to frequent the mall much more than in the past. When I entered as a freshman, only juniors and seniors could have cars and if you managed to finagle your away around the system to acquire a parking permit, your parking was probably far away in the woods somewhere. Now for the perks. Once I brought my car to campus, I wondered how I ever survived without it. Although there were increased costs that did create a new element of personal budgeting, the freedom was wonderful.

Leasing, financing, or buying a used car is your judgment call. I am usually not a fan of leasing, but leasing is cheaper than financing, and I have seen a couple of college students lease and they were happy with their decision. I would say buy new if you can afford to, or certified used. I had a lemon sold to me. (A lemon is a used car sold to you with several major defects that are not made known to you prior to purchasing it, that impairs the car from functioning normally). Over a two year span, I broke down on the side of a highway probably three times per year. Breaking down was not fun at all, but the freedom and flexibility of having a car still far outweighed the inconvenience of calling AAA and having my car towed.

It is a commitment to finance a car, so if you don't have a stable job or a good amount in savings, it may be too huge a commitment. If your parents are helping you, then great. Getting parking tickets or other traffic violations can be a hassle. Just follow the rules! The possibility of court, fines, points on your license, and increased insurance costs should deter you from breaking any rules. All in all, **despite the cost, I am an advocate of a car for the freedom it allows. You can go wherever you want to go, whenever you want to go.**

**14) E-mail/ IM/ Facebook/ MySpace/ Any other social networking site: Learn the art of turning off Instant**

**Messenger and checking Facebook and Myspace only once or twice a day as opposed to ten or twelve times.** You can end up spending hours of precious time on these activities. Unless you are expecting an important e-mail, set out a few moments during the day to briefly check and respond to e-mail. Be conscious of how much personal information you post on these sites, as well as uploading lewd pictures and inappropriate things of that nature.

**15) Your Family:** Be sure to connect with your family members through an occasional phone call or e-mail. Parents usually spend a great deal of time worrying about you and just want to know you are doing well.

When you go home for winter or summer break, your parents may not act the way you want them to. In college you are responsible for yourself. You can come home every night at three a.m. with no questions asked, but then when you're home on break, your mom may ask you to be home by one a.m. There seems to be something very wrong with this picture. Although it will suck, you must respect your parents and their home. Talk to them about it, but if they don't budge, **just follow their rules!**

**Side Note #22:** Make sure you buy a sweatshirt or another item of clothing to really represent your school when you're at home.

**Other family stuff:** This can include family-related drama like a family member being incarcerated, someone losing their job, or getting into some legal drama of your own. In Tip # 10 "Don't Be Too Hard On Yourself" I discuss utilizing the counseling center. If you get into a legal situation, utilize the free legal aid resources. If you remember anything I tell you, remember to use *all* the resources on campus that will aid in making your life easier and much more successful.

## So what did you learn about balance?

- Time management can become a game of trial and error until you figure out what really works for you.
- Study daily!
- Take your vitamins, eat properly, get enough sleep, and work out!
- Develop an exercise plan early on.
- Your goal should be to make exercise a part of your daily schedule.
- Try to minimize the length of your daily naps.
- Beware of germy sicknesses that are prevalent in college settings.
- Schedule your regular checkup at the health center, and if you are sick, be sure to go to the health center for treatment.
- STDs are real.
- Be sure to schedule activities that you enjoy and that put you at peace.
- If you get into credit card debt, commit to at least paying the minimum *on time* on a monthly basis.
- Save your money from summer jobs and internships.
- Try to do your laundry in the middle of the week and monitor the time your clothes are in the machines.
- Keep your room organized.
- Keep your hours at work to a minimum, meaning less than twenty hours a week.

- As you are conquering the world, remember to mind your own business and no one else's!
- Write down important dates and deadlines in your planner.
- Don't try to overkill your schedule with electives and procrastinate taking your major courses.
- Take classes that fit into your lifestyle.
- Do not plagiarize or cheat.
- Do not take nightly strolls on campus alone.
- Take a spring break trip every year that you can afford it.
- Bring along a friend or two to your partying sessions, especially when alcohol is involved.
- Study and do your work before you party.
- If you are going to live off campus, live within walking distance to campus public transportation.
- Having a car is great for the freedom it allows, but be aware of the car maintenance expenses.
- Learn the art of turning off Instant Messenger and checking your email, Facebook, and MySpace only once or twice a day as opposed to ten or twelve times.
- If your parents try to place restrictions on you over summer or winter break, talk to them about it, but if they do not budge, just follow their rules!

# The Last Days and Graduation: Enjoy the Moment!

Congratulations, you are a *soon-to-be* college graduate. You are moments away from entering the real world and making real money! **Senior year is one of the best years of your college experience!** Enjoy the moment!

But before you get too carried away, here is a quick dose of reality: **Until graduation day itself, and until you fulfill all of your college requirements, you have not earned your degree. You are not an alumnus just yet.** The college or university might allow you to walk across the stage and go through the procedures as if you have officially graduated, but you will not receive your diploma unless you pass all of your classes. If you are a few credits short of the requirement, you will have to pass a summer class or two before you earn your degree. What does all this mean? To officially graduate successfully, you have to do everything from Tip #1 to Tip #12, with an emphasis on the things most seniors think you are exempt from, such as studying and attending your classes. Furthermore, your GPA still matters, so **don't get comfortable and let your guard down.**

This is what makes senior year an interesting year. You still have tons of work to do, yet your enthusiasm and motivation gradually dwindles. You attempt to ride the year out until the school officials place the diploma in your hand. Unfortunately, you can not take that approach because senior year is still an important year. **Be sure to meet with your advisor in the beginning of the academic year to ensure that you are on the right track to fulfill all of the requirements to graduate on time. You should also have your post graduation plans well worked out.** If you are going to work after graduation, make sure you have a job or you have submitted your resume to several employers and have begun to schedule interviews. If you are going to graduate school, be sure you know the application requirements for the schools to which you plan to apply; you have identified and contacted those whom you are asking to write your letters of recommendation; and you have taken exam (e.g., GRE, GMAT, LSAT) review classes, have taken the exam, and are satisfied with your exam results.

**Side Note #1:** For those strongly considering graduate school after working two to five years, consider taking your graduate school entrance exam before you graduate college, while you are still in study mode. Scores usually last several years. For example, GMAT scores last five years. Also, know all the rules applicable for each exam. For example, there are certain certification exams, like the Certified Public Accountant (CPA) exam, that you can take as many times as you want. Then there are entrance exams like the LSAT's in which you should not take the exam as many times as you want. Taking the exam multiple times is not the best decision because not only are all your exam results averaged together, but schools look at taking these exams multiple times in an unfavorable manner.

Now let's talk about the senior year phases. The first phase is "the high." You go through an extreme high at the beginning of the year. During this high, you may get caught up in the fact that you're almost done. What most seniors fail to realize during this moment of bliss is that you still have a full year of classes to successfully complete. You may decide that this is the year to be bold and do all the things you have always wanted but were afraid to do. You've mustered up the courage to tell Darnell how much you've liked him ever since freshman year, even though he has a girlfriend. What do you have to lose? You're about to graduate! Right? Wrong. *Pump your brakes, girlfriend!* There is still a full year left of school. That equates to two sets of midterms, two sets of finals, and a bunch of other stuff in between, like group projects and probably some of the most difficult classes you have taken thus far in your college curriculum. And you will have to see Darnell's face for the rest of the year, so be wise about how much you want to confess to a guy who already has a girlfriend. So another reality check is: **You've come too far to flunk out and you've come too far to have your reputation go down the tubes.**

After the initial high in the beginning of the year comes phase two, or what is often termed "senioritis." Let me describe it a bit: You don't want to do any work or attend any classes. You've got this college thing pretty much down pact and know the art of not attending lectures, showing up only for exams, and still getting an A. You're invincible! You party nonstop, and have fun in a new and more mature way. Oh, and those itty bitty confused freshman; looking at them makes you realize how much you've grown.

**Side Note #2:** Senioritis can strike during your junior year or even worse, sophomore year. **Senioritis during any other year besides your senior year is dangerous!** When I was a junior, I had a friend who was a senior and I thought

I could live the same carefree lifestyle she was beginning to live. No way. Poor grades would impact my GPA more than hers. Additionally, junior year can be difficult because that is the year you start to really get into your major course requirements. You want to focus during this period of time. Keep in mind: If you are a junior, you are a junior. You are *not* a senior! Now let me continue talking to my real seniors.

After senioritis, there is phase three, called "reflection." You are excited and impressed. You realize what you've accomplished. You were able to pass that really difficult class and landed a job with a great starting salary. Then there is also the dark side of the reflection period. During this dark side, feelings of regret begin to creep in. You think, "By the time I graduated college, I wanted to accomplish x, y, and z and now it's too late." I want you to keep things in perspective. **Where you are now is where you are supposed to be.** Whatever it was that you thought you were supposed to accomplish may not have been for you, and it may be five, ten, twenty years or more that you will look back and see the reasoning behind it all. **At times the things you deem as failures have hidden learning lessons attached to them.**

Another point to keep in mind as you reflect is that **sometimes in the realm of college, things seem to be a much bigger deal than they really are.** Stop the pity party in its tracks. **Think about how much you have**

**accomplished!** I know you weren't just sleeping straight through those last couple of years. Try (and I know it's difficult) to be content in the state you are in. As much as we all wish, we cannot change the past. You are fabulous and graduating and there is a reason why you didn't do x, y, and z. It wasn't meant for you or the timing wasn't right. **There's probably something even bigger in store for you.** You just wait and see.

If there are things that you can change during your senior year, go ahead and change them. If you did not have any internship experience and are now looking for a job, get on your grind with securing a job offer! Refer back to Tip #6 on getting an internship and full-time job.

Another aspect of reflection is when you begin to question your direction in life. *What am I supposed to do? I want a job I'll love. I don't want to work a nine to five forever.* Many seniors question if they should get a job, go to graduate school, or work for a service organization like the Peace Corps or Teach for America. If others begin securing jobs and receiving acceptance letters into graduate school and you don't have either, you begin feeling even more down. Refer to Tip # 10 on not being too hard on yourself, particularly the segment on comparisons. When your high school peers begin graduating from college and you are taking a bit longer to earn your degree, you will feel down as well. Remember that everyone is different. Many people do not graduate in four years. Congratulate and be happy for them. Focus on what you need to do to graduate.

You know the mantra: "If at first you don't succeed, try and try again." **You are in control of your future. Never leave anything up to chance.** If you don't succeed the first time, figure out what went wrong and take active steps to change your situation. **You've come way too far to give up now.** Celebrate your accomplishment, and remember to *have fun!*

You have acquired lots of knowledge over the years and can better balance your time, so use this to your advantage during your senior year. **Instead of viewing this moment as a sad ending, think of it as a fabulous new beginning to a plethora of opportunities!**

## So what did you learn about senior year?

- Senior year is one of the best years of your college experience!
- Until graduation day itself, and until you have fulfilled all of your college requirements, you have not earned your degree. You are not an alumnus just yet.
- Don't get comfortable and let your guard down.
- You've come too far to flunk out and you've come too far to have your reputation go down the tubes.
- At times the things you deem as failures have hidden learning lessons attached to them.
- Sometimes in the realm of college, things seem to be a much bigger deal than they really are.
- Stop the pity party in its tracks. Be proud of all you have accomplished!
- Be content with your present situation.
- There's probably something even bigger in store for you.
- You are in control of your future. Never leave anything up to chance.
- You've come way too far to give up now.
- Have fun!
- Instead of viewing this moment as a sad ending, think of it as a fabulous new beginning to a plethora of opportunities!

# Tip #12: Did I Mention ... Have Fun?

There was a girl I knew in college named Michelle, who I always admired for having fun no matter what the circumstances were. No matter where she went or what she did, if you asked her, "So did you have fun?" the answer was always a hearty, "Yes, it was *so* much fun!" If it wasn't fun, she would be honest, but would still pull the good from the situation. If I asked someone else the same question, I would often hear the dull and melancholy, "Oh, it was okay," or that person would begin to ramble off all the things that went wrong. The point of the story: Michelle carried a great deal of optimism in her back pocket. There will be many times in college and in life when you will have to create the fun in your experience. Fun is an individual choice. Do what it takes to enjoy your college experience.

Really ladies, when everyone tells you "these are the best years of your life," believe them. Enjoy not having the full-time responsibilities of work, a family to take care of, and lots and lots of bills. Enjoy college! In the blink of an eye, it will be over. College is *fun*, but there is a great deal of work to do as well. You must put things into perspective. There is a specific reason why you are there and that is to get an education. The experience will happen on its own. If you got anything from this book, you should know that your education should be your top priority.

Have fun! Keep your GPA as high as possible! Get involved, as a volunteer at a soup kitchen, as a member of the Black Student Union, or as a member of a religious network. Transform yourself for the better, learn from the relationships you build, and have a good time while doing it. Have your post graduation plans in place before leaving the university. This could be having your job lined up, getting graduate school acceptance, or deferring a full-time offer to travel for a year. Have a plan! Whether your plans change or not, just have one!

In the introduction to this book I explained why I entitled the book *The Black Girl's Guide to College Success: What No One* Really *Tells You About College That You Must Know.* As you should know by now, college is more than studying and getting good grades. The college years, from the end of your teenage years to your early twenties, are a formidable period. It is when a girl really transforms into a woman. She is no longer sheltered from the realities of life and begins to define who she is and what she stands for. You start to really experience the roller coaster of life with little parental guidance. This is the time when you have to establish a balance like never before. You are forced to deal with the highs, lows, disappointments, and accomplishments of life; while still trying to uphold a high level of self-esteem and resilience in the process.

I wish I could include every single element of college life that you should be conscious of, but that would definitely take some of the fun out of the whole learning experience. As I stated in the "First Day Commandments," keep this book in a safe and accessible place because you will experience several of these issues and will need the advice I have presented. Last but not least, know that you are not alone, and in fact, you'll be more than okay. You will succeed! Work hard, ladies! You are fabulous, brilliant, and destined for success! It's now time to do your part!

Wishing you a very bright and prosperous future,

*Sheryl*

# ACKNOWLEDGEMENTS

I would like to thank God for helping me find the words to complete this book and blessing me with a fulfilling four years in college. I want to especially thank the following people for believing in my vision, helping with any editorial requests, and being supportive along the way:

Mom and Dad; my godmother Cecelia B. Gordon (R.I.P.); my sister Sophia; my brother Ricardo (and all of Ricardo's friends); my brother Dean; my niece and nephew Bailey and Mekhi; Angie; Aunts, Uncles, and Grandparents; Derrick; Shanell; Danielle, Mrs. Wilson, Mr. Wilson, twins, and extended Wilson family; The LaLa's: Reverend Christina, Natalie aka "Super Friend," Zenitra, Sydney; Joe; Devin; Gabi; Shonna; Vernedra; Mrs. Weatherspoon; friends and residents at the University of Maryland, College Park: Res Life, Friends of Lesotho, every past, present, and future member of BBA and NABA;

Omoniyi; Kaya; Crystal; Marae; Ashley; The twelve girls I lived with as an RA; The entire First Church family of Teaneck: Pastor Montcrieffe, Bernard, The Goulding's, The Richards', The Gordon's: Gram, Len, Yvette, Xavier, and Cyrus; Formal and informal mentors during internships and jobs: Roy, Tim, Kim, Elena, Rosalind, Lukeman, Raheem, Kathy-Ann, Kerri, Shari, and Maida; Lakshmi (INROADS NY); Erin Turner-Byfield; Michael Abdul-Qawi; My high school and college English teachers: Ms. Farley, Ms. Norton, Mr. Rosner, Ms. Lombardi, and Marybeth Shea; The original *Black Girl's Guide* street team; Also- any friend I forgot to mention that is listed as a friend on Facebook or MySpace.

To those I have failed to mention, it is the fault of my head, not my heart. This book is to all the fabulous men and women in my life. You have all inspired me!

# About the Author:

Sheryl Walker graduated high school as the third in her class and the highest ranked African-American student. She received several scholarships and honors, including the English department's Creative Writing Award.

Sheryl attended the University of Maryland in College Park where she was admitted into the College Park Scholars International Studies Colloquium. She graduated with a B.S. degree in accounting in May 2005. She served as president for the National Association of Black Accountants (NABA) chapter, as a resident assistant, and as vice president of membership for the Black Business Association (BBA). She received recognition from the Office of Multi-Ethnic Student Education during several semesters as well as the Minority Scholars 2004 Accounting Scholarship, National Association of Black Accountants DC Metro Chapter 2004 Scholarship, and the Omega Psi Phi Fraternity Incorporated 2004 Essay Scholarship. Sheryl also studied abroad in South Africa and Lesotho during the winter term of her senior year.

Sheryl had four internships and also held a part-time job on campus during her senior year. She was involved with the Caribbean Student Association, was a staff writer for the campus newspaper *The Eclipse*, and was a mentor with the Black Student Union. Her community involvement included walking in various walks for AIDS and diabetes, as well as serving lunch to the homeless on a monthly basis.

Sheryl is now working for a public accounting firm in New York and writes in her leisure. The *Black Girl's Guide To College Success: What No One* Really *Tells You About College That You Must Know* is the first of a series of *Black Girl's Guides* to come.

Printed in the United States
122410LV00001B/83/A